The Effective Management
of
Volunteer Programs

by

Marlene Wilson

Published by
Volunteer Management Associates
279 South Cedar Brook Road
Boulder, Colorado 80302

Printed by
Johnson Publishing Company
Boulder, Colorado

Foreword

A rare combination of humane and very efficient management perspectives characterize this practical guide to volunteer management. Warm and humorous illustrations from practice brighten sound theories of management. The most universally expressed learning need in the volunteer world is for just such practical help for people making a career of matching volunteers to places where they are needed. One of the best of these practitioners shares her insights from serious study of business management theory, practice as an administrator and university mentor.

Increasingly, human service agencies are being held accountable for gifts of time, effort and money (tax or donation) and the use of talents as well as essential materials. Good management of volunteers is important for the generally underpaid, overworked staff, from executive down to the newest employee. To have and to hold appropriate, dependable helpers takes planning, preparation, organizing and overseeing, with constant concern for individuality. Patients, tutees, or whatever label we give the consumers or recipients of the volunteer services are the most important people in the hierarch of those to be considered. Volunteer managers must insure that they have a good experience and relationships with their volunteers which reinforce and extend their use of the agency services.

It is not easy to achieve order and maintain the essential freedoms of choice for volunteers about what they do, and for others about

3

which volunteer fits in most harmoniously. Order instead of chaos, like good housekeeping, makes life more comfortable and productive. Yet response to well meant spontaneity means responsibility for appreciation of volunteer intentions, steering enthusiasm into priority channels. Enabling volunteers to apply their fullest potential and to continue developing more takes a high degree of skill, sensitivity and flexibility. When volunteering was limited to the already over-privileged, who were seeking recreation and socializing, no one took it seriously.

Most people have altruistic reasons for volunteering with a healthy streak of self-interest. But the possibilities for real social action, community change agentry, new roles for older persons, career exploration for the young mean that volunteers now come in all sizes, ages, shapes and backgrounds. Gaps in support, lack of evaluation of impact, pedagogical training, which limited the homogeneous constituency, are simply intolerable with a pluralistic constituency of volunteers.

There is a lag in realizing what a wide range of skills and knowledge is now required for volunteer management, except among the people trying to do it! Marlene Wilson shows the differences in behavioral terms: more active reaching out, bridging communication gaps and helping people with few similar experiences or objectives to find their commonalities. If pluralism in a democratic society is to survive, token use of volunteers is as destructive to the individual as low priority for voluntarism is to our society.

Keeping volunteers interested and growing means offering people a life-long learning opportunity which will keep them in touch with the mainstream issues of the day. With revenue sharing pushing decision making responsibilities back to the local community, citizens need to understand the needs and weigh the resources available. Community problems are multiplying while resources are shrinking. The average citizen will have to learn how to make choices about priorities. He cannot ignore the needs of victims of economic, health or social disasters when he knows them as persons and has worked shoulder to shoulder on a community project.

Volunteering can mean self-renewal for the volunteer and for the community. But only with the kind of leadership Marlene Wilson describes will citizens stick with volunteering long enough to make a difference. Her values are rooted in a deep concern for what happens to people. The evolving occupation of volunteer management is unique in that it channels compassion, "humanizes" the quality of life, gives access to the process of effecting change. Best of all, it means sharing enjoyment of the best side of human nature. She has given us the *how-to's* and the *whys*. Now we must each find our own *where* and *what* to practice as she preaches!

Harriet H. Naylor
Washington, D.C.

Preface

This book is intended to be practical, rather than academic or theoretical. It is a sharing of a basic philosophy about people and how to treat them in a way that encourages growth and self-renewal in individuals and organizations.

Directors of volunteer programs have both an awesome responsibility and unique opportunity to bring about constructive change in the organizations and communities in which they work. However, it requires more than just good will and dedication. It involves management skills of the highest order.

Therefore, I have sought to expose the reader to the rich array of literature from the fields of business and management, the behavioral sciences and communications available to enrich our understanding and functioning in this field.

I make no claim that much of the material is new or original thinking on my part. What I have attempted to do is utilize my years of experience in personnel administration and volunteer management to apply management theory to a volunteer program and make it work. I speak as one practitioner to others, having shared the same struggles of the day-to-day operation of a volunteer program. Almost everything suggested has been trial tested in our own program and found to be both possible and useful.

My overarching goal in these pages is to confront honestly the impact we, as managers of volunteer programs, have on the people who work with and for us. Managers either enrich or diminish others. So the question remains—what are *we* doing to people?

I am deeply indebted to the many who enabled me. My husband, Harvey, a corporation Vice President of Personnel and Administration, served as chief resource, critic and supplier of the extensive library that proved invaluable. My children, Rich and Lisa, patiently and enthusiastically provided encouragement from the sidelines. It is to Harvey, Rich and Lisa that I lovingly dedicate this book.

Inspiration and counsel were provided by Dr. Ivan Scheier, Harriet Naylor and Dr. David Horton Smith. These three people have greatly influenced me and I admire them deeply. They, together with Gay Beattie and Ruth Hattendorf, were kind enough to read and make suggestions on parts or all of the book.

The book would not have been possible without the volunteers on my Advisory Committees (past and present) who have helped me learn and grow with them. My secretary, Barbara Taylor Green carried a great deal of extra responsibility at the Volunteer and Information Center during the writing of this book.

And finally, to Virginia Swartz, the finest typist I know—my deepest gratitude.

Marlene Wilson

Table of Contents

This Chapter examines some of the vast changes that are occuring in this field, and what these changes dictate regarding the changing role of the manager of volunteer programs. Attitudes and philosophies are explored as they affect the effective vs. token use of volunteers. The intent is to explode the old theory that "anyone can run a volunteer program," and to develop a sense of urgency on the part of managers of volunteer programs to seek training and develop skills needed to do the job that needs doing.

Those directing volunteer programs must be confronted with the fact that they are indeed managers and as such they must both understand and accept that responsibility. The functions of a manager, as outlined by Koontz and O'Donnell, (planning, organizing, staffing, directing and controlling) are explained. Leadership in relationship to management is examined and some emphasis placed on the affect management style has on the climate and effectiveness of an organization.

The question of why people volunteer is dealt with especially as this relates to successful placement and retention of volunteers. Various theories of motivation are presented, with particular emphasis being given to David McClelland's research regarding motivation.

The effect the climate of an organization has on both volunteers and staff is dealt with, again in light of McClelland's research, as well as that of Rensis Likert. A measurement tool is presented to help an organization assess its climate and suggestions made as to implementing changes that may be dictated by the assessment. The relationship of management style to organizational climate is reinforced.

Some information on Management by Objectives and the goal setting process is covered. The intent is to encourage the reader to assess their own program's needs and to design systems to meet those needs. Evaluation is presented as a necessary adjunct and component of planning.

This Chapter traces the logical sequence of recruitment for both paid and volunteer jobs from assessing needs, to creative job design and culminates in suggested recruiting techniques and approaches. The concept of volunteer leaders, or volunteer "professionals" is also covered.

The intent is to give the reader concrete tools to assist them in their efforts of getting the right person into the right job. Some of the topics dealt with are registration forms, interviewing techniques (screening and in-depth interviews), matching, referral procedures and follow up techniques. The goal is to help people discover and deal with the needs, aspirations and skills of the volunteer and not just the needs of the agency.

These three phases of training are included:

—Training Volunteer Directors
—Training Volunteers
—Training Staffs to Work With Volunteers

Emphasis is placed on andragogy (adult learning) vs. pedagogy (child learning). Rather than presenting training models, the basic philosophy and methodologies are explored.

The complexity of the communications requirements of Directors of Volunteers will be examined —the necessity of communicating with administration, staff, volunteer, client and community. Communications is viewed as a process of meaning creating rather than idea or message sending. It is essential that managers learn to build and free people instead of destroy or diminish them.

The unique and individual role of each component of the organization is examined. The challenge is to blend all of the unique and essential parts into a whole greater than the parts (synergism). Trust is the essential ingredient and self renewal of the person and the organization the goal.

CHAPTER I

A New Look at Volunteerism

There is a legend in the Middle East about a spindly little sparrow lying on his back in the middle of the road. A horseman comes by, dismounts and asks the sparrow what he's doing lying upside down like that.

"I heard the heavens are going to fall today," said the sparrow.

"Oh," said the horseman, "and I suppose your spindly little legs can hold up the heavens."

"One does what one can," said the sparrow. "One does what one can!"

Those of us engaged in the field of social services must sometimes appear to be like this little sparrow, wishfully thinking that somehow we are going to be able to stem the tide of human need. And the horsemen of our day come riding by and point out how our spindly efforts will never keep the weight of population, urbanization, polarization and pollution from eventually crushing the life out of all of us.

And yet most of us would emphatically echo the little sparrow . . . one does what one can! And in my opinion, the size of the challenge we face today simply points out the need for us to continue doing what we can to help alleviate human need, but to do it much better.

I am afraid there has traditionally been a tendency on the part of those engaged in social (or human) services, to look with scepticism on other disciplines, at least when it came to the possibility of learning anything from them. Today, with the complexities and immensity of the problems before us we can no longer afford that luxury.

We are witnessing and experiencing the evolution of a whole new and exciting career on the social services scene, that of volunteer management or administration. I believe it is up to those of us engaged in this career to consciously decide from the very beginning that our jobs are truly inter-disciplinary in scope and that we will not only eagerly accept, but actively seek out knowledge, methods and techniques from any other field that will help us do our jobs more effectively.

The job we have before us is an urgent and significant one, for many social scientists and observers of human affairs tell us that the helping spirit is a rapidly dying phenomenon in 1975 America. We are in the midst of a recession, disturbingly reminiscent of the 1930 depression, where the unemployment rate is soaring. Needs for human services are increasing at an alarming rate and resources to meet those needs are decreasing as cities, states, and the federal government tighten their fiscal belts. One New York columnist recently observed that it is now a time when it's everyone for himself and illustrated this with examples of municipal workers being willing to let New York go bankrupt rather than take minimum wage cuts or give up fringe benefits.

However, not all people agree with this pessimism about the helping spirit today. According to national statistics volunteerism is increasing steadily. The latest Census Bureau study regarding volunteerism states "helping others" is the primary motive for 53% of the estimated 37 million Americans who volunteer, and that percentage is on the increase. (See Chapter III.) What is changing is the kind of people who volunteer and the modes of helping. This speaks directly to our responsibilities as Directors of volunteer efforts.

Professional workers in human service agencies face the mandate of those in need to deliver services more effectively and the thousands of volunteers who serve within these agencies must examine their efforts as well. Somehow we as a nation need to rekindle the creative energies of volunteers to not just help carry out the services

14

of existing agencies, but to be the pace-setters once again in helping find new solutions to old problems.

George Romney issues the challenge. "In every community and every state across the country we need to program for voluntary action by the people, not just government action for the people—many problems can be tackled right at home, human and social problems like education, mental illness, traffic safety, urban decay, crime, delinquency, and family deterioration, through the organization of voluntary effort. Nothing can melt such human and social problems faster than the willingness of one individual to involve himself voluntarily in helping another individual overcome his problems."[1]

The key to Mr. Romney's statement in my opinion, is the phrase *"organization of voluntary effort"*. Obviously, volunteers have involved themselves in meeting the needs of communities for as long as we have existed as a nation. It's sort of a quirk of our national character. What we are just beginning to realize is that as our communities grow and the problems increase and become more complex, helping one's neighbor becomes more complex as well. Idealistic good intentions often backfire and sincere volunteers are disillusioned as they "burn themselves out" in good causes that all too frequently seem to go nowhere.

Often these problems occur because the voluntary effort was not organized effectively. I suggest that our communities can no longer afford the luxury of good programs and good people that fail. We need to objectively look at these failures and ask *why* and then set about doing something about it.

It is my opinion, based on dozens of consultations, workshops, seminars and conversations concerning volunteer programs, that there is one common denominator in an amazing number of volunteer programs experiencing difficulty. It is not the volunteers, nor the client, but the person directing the volunteer program. This seems ironic, for I have yet to meet a group that works harder to help people or is more idealistic and dedicated.

Let us look at some of the probable causes of this problem. How frequently is the job of Director of Volunteers (or Coordinator, Administrator, or Supervisor of Volunteers) regarded so lightly by social service agencies that it is haphazardly delegated to any staff person who has some free time? It is assumed that he or she will absorb these new responsibilities on a part time basis, while continuing other assignments. Often there is little, if any, training provided to prepare the person for the job and the commitment received from agency administration and other staff members is all too often hazy and sporadic. And it is not uncommon for the salary paid to this person to reflect the philosophy that the person directing volunteers should be willing to donate much of the time it takes to do so. It is frequently difficult to ascertain if this assignment should be regarded as a promotion or demotion.

It is no wonder many Volunteer Directors have difficulty accepting the fact that they are, in fact, managers of very important programs and as such need to develop the expertise to be *good managers*.

But it is imperative that we face this responsibility. Our volunteers and communities deserve no less. In *Management of Organizational Behavior: Utilizing Human Resources*, the authors point out, "The successful organization has one major attribute that sets it apart from unsuccessful organizations—dynamic and effective leadership . . . we have plenty of administrative 'bodies'. What we are agonizing over is a scarcity of people who are willing to assume significant leadership roles in our society, and can get the job done effectively."[2] And why should this be any less important if our work forces are *unpaid rather than paid,* and if our organizations are engaged in *human services rather than industry?* I submit it makes it even more important.

One of the most provocative and exciting statements I have encountered on leadership is an essay entitled *The Servant As Leader* by Robert Greenleaf. The author suggests that a new moral principle is emerging in this country. This principle holds that the only authority deserving one's allegiance is that which is freely and knowingly granted by the led to the leader in response to, and in proportion to the clearly evident "servant status" of the leader. "They will freely respond only to individuals who are chosen as leaders because they are proven and trusted servants."[3] The test of the servant-leader is what has happened to those served under their leadership—have they grown or diminished, become freer or more enslaved?

He goes on to lay the blame for the deterioration and difficulties of our troubled society where it, in my estimation, belongs. "The real enemy is fuzzy thinking on the part of good, intelligent, vital people, and their failure to lead . . . too many settle for being critics and experts. There is too much intellectual wheel spinning, too much

16

retreating into 'research', too little preparation for and willingness to undertake the hard and high risk tasks of building better institutions in an imperfect world . . . *in short, the enemy is strong natural servants who have the potential to lead, but do not lead.*"[4]

There are many people in the field of human services who are recognizing the tremendously significant role that Directors of volunteer programs have to play in today's world.

Dr. Tessie Okin, Professor of the School of Social Administration, Temple University, in an address given for the Association of Volunteer Bureaus, Inc. in May 1973 stated:

"Modern volunteers are a unique breed whose ancestors helped build this country. Their potential is incalculable. Key persons on the American scene, closely involved with the volunteer citizen in action are the Directors of Volunteers, a group moving toward professionalism. *The largest impact on masses of citizen volunteers may be had through appropriately training Directors of Volunteers.*"[4]

Dr. Ivan Scheier, Director of the National Information Center on Volunteerism, recently stated that volunteer program administration is just emerging as an exciting profession which partakes of many traditional disciplines, though it is owned by none of them.

And what about the work force that this emerging profession is charged with leading? A Census Bureau survey conducted in April, 1974 indicates there were approximately 37 million Americans over 14 volunteering at that time. Others estimate that figure to be as high as 50-70 million. The U. S. Department of Labor in its Manpower/Automation Research Monograph, *Americans Volunteer*, estimate that by 1980 the volunteer work force will contribute $30 billion annually to the U.S. economy (figured as part of the gross national product).

To verify how the field of volunteerism is growing, a look at some statistics on a local, state and national level may prove helpful. Specific programs in Colorado have been used since no current statistics are available for the field in general. Similar growth patterns are reflected across the country and in Canada.

A. LOCAL PROGRAMS

1. *The Volunteer & Information Center of Boulder County (VIC).* This center was organized 7 years ago to recruit and place volunteers with social service agencies in Boulder. The first year

there were 35 agencies seeking volunteers through this agency. Currently 80 agencies list over 450 varieties of volunteer opportunities. Over 5000 volunteers have been recruited and placed in Boulder through VIC in these 7 years. And the demand for volunteers continues to increase steadily.

2. *Mental Health Center of Boulder.* This Boulder volunteer program has experienced phenomenal growth during the past nine years. In 1966 they had 15 volunteers and by 1975, this had grown to 350. The Executive Director at one time estimated the monetary value of these volunteers as being $12,000 per month, due to the fact that many of their volunteers are professionals and graduate students.

3. *Clearing House.* The volunteer bureau for students at the University of Colorado estimates they had 1,100-1,200 students involved as volunteers in their 20 programs during 1974-75.

4. *Denver Public Schools.* The Volunteer Coordinator reports that 6,436 volunteers were utilized in 105 of Denver's public schools during the past two years (only 16 schools did not use volunteers). There are 23 separate volunteer programs represented in these figures. This same growth pattern of school volunteer programs is occuring across the nation with Right-to-Read, Community Study Halls, tutor programs, learning disability programs, etc., emerging rapidly. These programs are designed to correct and hopefully prevent the appalling statistics that 16-18 million Americans over 16 are illiterate.

5. *Denver Metro Volunteer Administrator's Association.* This association is approximately 2 years old and includes Denver, Arapahoe, Adams and Jefferson Counties' Volunteer Administrators. There are 250 agencies with organized volunteer programs listed with this Association, and over one-half of these have salaried Volunteer Administrators. The others utilize volunteers for this purpose.

B. Colorado State-Wide Programs

1. *Department of Public Welfare.* During the past four years, 26 county welfare departments have established volunteer programs. (There were none prior to 1970.) Some of these programs have full-time-paid Coordinators, and others have part-time staff.

2. *Court Programs.* There are 25 court volunteer programs in Colorado. This figure has tripled in the past three years.

3. *Retired Senior Volunteer Program* (RSVP). Thirteen new programs funded by ACTION for volunteers over 60 have been established in Colorado during the past two years. (Nine of these started during a two month period late in 1973.)

C. NATIONAL PROGRAMS

1. *ACTION Volunteer Programs*

a. Retired Senior Volunteer Program (RSVP) has the following national figures:

> June 1971—11 programs—0 volunteers
> June 1972—80 programs—1,500 volunteers
> Dec. 1973—590 programs—63,205 volunteers
> June 1974—662 programs—101,612 volunteers

The federal government has invested $18.5 million in this program and funds are being increased next year.

b. VISTA. As of June, 1974 there were 443 VISTA projects in the U. S. involving 4,327 volunteers.

c. University Year for Action. Fifty-five projects were established by June 1974 with 1,715 volunteers.

d. Foster Grandparents. 12,193 seniors are involved in this national program.

2. *National Center for Voluntary Action (NCVA)*. Over 200 Voluntary Action Centers have been established across the country during the past three years and NCVA is hoping to greatly increase this number during the bicentennial year.

3. *Court Programs.* Seventy per cent of all juvenile courts and 10 per cent of all adult courts in the U. S. now have organized volunteer programs. There were only four such programs in 1961. There are 80 professionals hired to do state-wide coordination of court programs (a position that did not exist 3-4 years ago). Each of the local programs also has a paid or volunteer Administrator.

4. And during the past two years 23 states have obtained ACTION grants, and added governor-appointed *State Offices of Volunteers* to help coordinate and facilitate voluntary efforts at the state level.

Another significant development has been the formation of national associations in this field. In the May, 1973, issue of *Voluntary*

Action News it stated, "the development of volunteer associations during the past decade reflects a growing maturity in the volunteer movement." Some of these associations are:

> *The Association of Volunteer Bureaus*
> *American Association of Volunteer Service Coordinators*
> *American Society of Directors of Volunteers Services of the*
> *American Hospital Association*
> *Association of Voluntary Action Scholars*
> *International Association for Volunteer Education*
> *National School Volunteer Program, etc.*

And a movement that is just currently beginning is for some of these national associations and organizations to form into coalitions.

One of the largest of these, the Alliance for Volunteerism, Inc., was formed in 1975 and encompasses eleven national organizations: National Center for Voluntary Action, National Information Center on Volunteerism, Call for Action, Association of Volunteer Bureaus, American Association of Volunteer Service Coordinators, Association of Voluntary Action Scholars, Involvement Corps, Volunteers in Technical Assistance, Black United Way, Church Women United and the Federation of Negro Women. ACTION is representing the public sector as a non-voting member. They are directing their efforts toward shared task forces addressing the common concerns of the field, such as education, standards, research, advocacy for voluntarism, technical assistance, etc.

So it would seem that more people than ever are volunteering and they represent all segments of the community. Blue collar workers, students, retired professional people, businessmen, office workers, clients . . . have all joined with housewives to swell the ranks of community action groups of all kinds. The skills required to direct the activities of such a large and diverse group are much more exacting than those needed a few years ago, when volunteering was still the uncomplicated process of "helping out."

The volunteers today are struggling to become involved in the deeper issues of society as well. Dr. Sanford Kravitz, Dean of the School of Social Welfare of the State University of New York, brought the issue into sharp focus when he said:

> "It is no longer enough to bandage social wounds and heal the sick. Inequality must become equality; injustice must be changed to justice. The job of each and every concerned vol-

20

unteer citizen is to find the right which fits the wrong of every aggrieved person in this society. Can the concerned voices and actions of thousands of volunteers be a part of such a movement?"[5]

The volunteers of today certainly think so, and this becomes another part of the challenge to the Volunteer Director—to see that the *informed* voices of volunteers are heard and acted upon. Volunteers have both the opportunity and the responsibility to become society's value changers if they are utilized effectively. And the grievous problems our communities face today desperately need this kind of positive attention. Never before in our history has citizen input not only been allowed, but actually mandated by so many governmental programs. From Headstart to Revenue Sharing—from mental health to senior programs—from comprehensive health programs to the Community Development Act—community and citizen input is not only requested, but required. It is the volunteers we are training today who can give informed and humane counsel to these programs tomorrow. *It must happen,* or communities will continue to make bad decisions about human service priorities by default, if not by design.

Yet there are serious counterforces at work making this task of finding and training volunteers more difficult. The Women's Liberation movement has taken national stands against service volunteering for women (although they endorse "change volunteering"). Some labor unions are negotiating to keep the free labor of volunteers out of their jurisdictions (i.e., schools), and societal and economic pressures are enticing more and more women into the paid work force as opposed to the volunteer ranks. So issues that have never before confronted this field are doing so now, and the importance and immensity of the job to be done demands that we deal with them.

Would you agree then, that volunteer administration is a key function of a vital activity in a changing world? Harriet Naylor in her fine book, *Volunteers Today: Finding, Training and Working With Them,* describes it very colorfully, "It takes a remarkable combination of enthusiasm, flexibility, sensitivity and courage . . . people who can not survive an atmosphere of ambiguity and confusion should not attempt to manage a volunteer program".[6]

So the challenge is clear! But the question remains, *how* do we become effective managers of volunteer programs? Hopefully this book will begin to grapple with that question.

My first premise in dealing with the issue is that what we are engaged in is a profession that is truly interdisciplinary in scope. It requires our willingness to break through the traditional sanctity of the social services to search out what we might learn from other fields. Certainly there is much we need to know encompassed in sociology and psychology, but let us also include appropriate skills and wisdom from communications, business administration and the behavioral sciences. After all, we need all the help we can get to "do good and do well" at the same time.

My intent is to combine topics unique to the field of volunteer administration with those things encompassed in other disciplines, that speak most directly to our needs. If we can learn how to recruit *good* volunteers, design *meaningful* jobs for them to do, interview and place each one *carefully* and create a climate in our agencies that allows them to function *effectively* and *creatively*—just think of the astounding inroads we can make into the problems that confront our communities today!

However a frustrating reality has existed in the past for those Directors of Volunteers who have seriously wanted more training. It has been almost impossible to get, except through occasional short seminars or single courses offered at a few colleges or universities. Until very recently virtually no institution of higher learning in the country has recognized the needs of this burgeoning new field of volunteer administration.

A few are beginning to address it. Some examples are: the University of Colorado in Boulder, which initiated a 9 course Certification Program for Volunteer Management in January 1974, through the Department of Continuing Education, (and is in the process of defining a degreed program with a speciality in Vol. Administration); Lincoln State University in Illinois offers a B.A. in Volunteer Administration, while Sacramento State College, University of Denver, Southern Illinois University, Springfield College, Massachusetts, Missouri Valley College, North Carolina State, University of Pittsburgh, Gavilan College in California, Virginia Commonwealth University, Eastern Washington State College, Highline Community College in Washington, and Salem College in West Virginia, all offer one or more courses for credit in volunteer administration.

Goddard College in Plainfield, Vermont offers external degree programs at the B.A. and M.A. levels on an independent study basis; some Universities Without Walls are recognizing practical experience in the field as applying toward accreditation; and, there is currently a surge of other colleges, universities, community colleges and junior colleges who are either adding single courses in volunteer administration or extending the ones they presently have.

The National Information Center on Volunteers has received a grant from Lilly Foundation to establish a National Learning Resource Center for the purpose of compiling information on all present learning opportunities in this field, to assist perspective students in locating such opportunities and to help extend and increase the present options. For information write NICOV at 1221 University Avenue, Boulder, Colorado 80302.

We have not yet arrived academically—but there is hope! Now it behooves those of us in the field to not only take advantage of the new training opportunities, but to have a hand in developing them as well.

This is truly an exciting time to be engaged in this field. What has been an undefined profession for a good many years is emerging at this moment in time. It has been there for years, but now we are finally seeing that it has an entity, professional stature, literature and character all its own.

If the job seems somewhat overwhelming, may we rest with the knowledge that it is worth the best we have to offer. As John Gardner said, "Leaders can conceive and articulate goals that lift people out of their petty preoccupations, carry them above the conflicts that tear a society apart, and unite them in the pursuit of objectives worthy of their best efforts".[7] It is such leaders that the volunteers of today desperately need . . . and deserve.

References

1. Romney, George, quoted in *The Volunteer Community*, Schindler-Rainman, Eva & Lippitt, Ronald, NTL Learning Resources, Inc., 1971, p. 15.
2. Hersey, Paul and Blanchard, Kenneth H., *Management of Organizational Behavior*, Prentice-Hall, Inc., 1972-69, p. 67.
3. Greenleaf, Robert, *The Servant As Leader*, Center for Applied Studies, 17 Dunster Street, Cambridge, Mass., 1972, p. 4.
4. Ibid, p. 35.
5. Report of the 1973 Association of Volunteer Bureaus Conference.
6. Naylor, Harriet H., *Volunteers Today: Finding, Training, and Working With Them*, Dryden Assoc., 1967-73, p. 190.
7. Gardner, John W., *The Anti-Leadership Vaccine* (1965 Annual report, The Carnegie Corp. of New York).

CHAPTER II

The Role of a Manager

It would be interesting to ask the man or woman you meet on the street what mental image comes to mind when they hear the term "manager." One might think of a bank executive, another the person who manages her apartment building and still another the person in charge of their Little League baseball team. They also could legitimately refer to ministers, generals, housewives . . . and Volunteer Administrators or Directors.

A widely accepted definition of the term manager is *someone who works with and through others to accomplish organizational goals.* The organization can be an industry, church, agency, voluntary organization or any other group of people who have organized themselves in order to get something accomplished.

Peter Drucker in his book, *The Practice of Management,* states "A manager does his work by getting other people to do theirs" and to illustrate this, he point out that IBM defines the manager's job as assistant to his subordinates.[1] In other words *a good manager is an enabler of human resources.*

Since we, as Directors of Volunteer Programs, do work with and through other people (both paid and non-paid people) to accomplish the goals of our agencies and programs, we are, in fact, managers. It is up to us to recognize this fact and assume the responsibility of becoming the best managers we possibly can.

However, I have sensed a reluctance on the part of many Directors to either recognize or deal with this issue. Perhaps past experience has conditioned them to equate the term manager with "boss" or "manipulator." It is important to understand that the term itself simply defines a function, and is therefore neither good nor bad. It is how a person carries out that function that matters. The important thing for those directing volunteer programs is to understand the impact they have on the lives of others—volunteers, staff and clients —and to take that responsibility seriously.

Nicholas Murry Butler, former president of Columbia University, once observed that people can be classed into three major categories. There is a small group of people who make things happen. There is a somewhat larger group of people who watch things happen, and there is an overwhelming majority of the people who don't have the slightest idea what is happening . . . The innovative manager is a person who makes things happen.

It is interesting to note that he did not say all managers, but only innovative managers belong in his first category. Perhaps a worthwhile goal for Directors of Volunteers is to become the sort of leaders who *make things happen,* both in our volunteer programs and in our communities at large.

But I would suggest we extend that goal even further by becoming the type of managers who can encourage and enable others we work with, both paid staff and volunteers, to become doers and movers as well. The future of our communities and country lies with those who are no longer content to be placid observers, but who are determined to become origins instead of pawns of the future. It is a challenging task we set for ourselves.

Robert Townsend, former President of Avis Rent-A-Car, in his well known book *Up the Organization,* gives us the key when he observes "things get done in our society because of a man or woman with conviction."[2] Are we convinced of the value of our volunteer programs and if so, do other people sense that conviction? If we are personally committed to what we are doing, others will be drawn to those programs who will soon want them to succeed as desperately as we do, and those people are called *volunteers.*

Mr. Townsend also stated that "good organizations are living bodies that grow new muscles to meet challenges."[3] If this is true of organizations, then it would also seem to apply to those who lead organizations—the managers. By learning as much as possible about the skills, functions and various styles of management, we should be able to discover where our managerial muscles are flabby, or non-existent. Once we know that, it is possible to set about strengthening ourselves and our organizations.

One of the first things it is important to realize is that there is no single role of a manager, but rather a complex of many different roles. The effectiveness of a manager depends on his or her flexibility to respond appropriately to varying situations and diverse people.

Douglas McGregor, in *The Human Side of Enterprise,* points out there are times when a manager finds it appropriate to be the leader of a group of subordinates, or a member of a group of his peers, or a teacher, decision maker, disciplinarian, helper, consultant, or simply an observer.[4]

For the volunteer program Director, it is essential to be genuinely sensitive to what is appropriate based on the situation and people involved. Inflexibility is the greatest weakness of many managers. We must have solid peer relationships with other paid staff in the agency (and other agencies); be teacher, helper, decision-maker, and, if need be, disciplinarian to the volunteers; leader or consultant as the expert in our field for that agency. It is essential we not become rigid in any of these roles, but feel comfortable with them all.

All too frequently when we fail to achieve the results we want, we look for the causes everywhere but the right place. Frequently it is our inappropriate managerial methods. It is much easier to blame others, such as "those incapable secretaries" or the "unreliable volunteers".

Being a good manager or leader is not easy in today's world of bureaucracies and complex organizations. In the *Peter Principle,* Peter & Hull state, "Most hierarchies are nowadays so cumbered with rules and traditions, and so bound in by public laws, that even high employees do not have to lead anyone anywhere, in the sense of pointing out the direction and setting the pace. They simply follow precedents, obey regulations, and move at the head of the crowd. Such employees lead only in the sense that the carved wooden figurehead leads the ship".[5]

But we have set for ourselves the goal of being the kind of managers who make things happen, so we must at all costs keep the existence of bureaucratic mediocrity from diverting us or diluting our intentions to attain the strength that comes from competency. Let us proceed then to learn from those who lead well.

According to Peter Drucker in his book, *The Effective Executive,* there are five practices or habits of mind that most good executives and managers possess.[6]

1. *They know where their time goes.* They control it rather than vice versa, by analyzing where it is going and then organizing it so it can and will be productive. They try to:

   —identify and eliminate things that are just busy work—things that no one will really miss if they go undone. (A friend of mine calls these things "administrivia");

   —decide what they could delegate to someone else;

   —identify "time wasters" such as unproductive meetings and unnecessary memos, and try to eliminate them.

2. *They focus on outward contribution.* In other words, they concentrate on results rather than just the work itself. As Drucker says, they look up from their work and outward toward goals. The manager lives and acts in two time dimensions for he "not only has to prepare for crossing distant bridges, he has to build them long before he gets there".

3. *They build on strengths, not weaknesses.* This includes not only their own strengths, but those of their superiors, colleagues and subordinates. They acknowledge and accept their own strengths and weaknesses, and they are able to accept the best in others without being threatened. They also recognize that they have the opportunity and responsibility to help others grow. They "feed opportunities and starve problems."

4. *They concentrate on the few major areas where superior performance will produce outstanding results* . They do this by setting and sticking to priorities. Some guidelines Drucker suggests in setting priorities are:

   —pick the future as opposed to the past;

   —focus on opportunity rather than problems;

   —choose your own direction instead of hearing someone else's drummer; and

—aim high and for something that makes a difference instead of limiting your goals to only the safe and easy things. Be an innovator.

5. *They make effective, rational decisions.* There are certain steps most effective managers go through in decision-making:

a) define the problem;

b) analyze the problem;

c) develop alternative solutions;

d) decide on the best solution; and

e) convert the decision into effective action.

Let us try this formula out on a typical problem in a volunteer program. An older, established mental health agency discovers it no longer has nearly enough volunteers to meet the growing needs of their clients. Many requests for volunteers are not being filled and the Director of Volunteers is being criticized by staff and administration for not doing a good job.

In analyzing the problem we might find: 1) there has been inadequate recruitment efforts; 2) volunteer turnover has increased; 3) staff is not supervising volunteers appropriately; 4) there has been little or no public relations about the volunteer program the past six months; 5) there is no longer training provided for volunteers due to increased workloads of staff; or 6) the public image of this agency is negative. Any or all of these factors could contribute to the problem and the task is to determine which of them are present in this particular situation.

Developing alternatives would need to be directly related to what was discovered in the problem analysis. For example, if the major problem was ineffective recruitment, some alternatives would be to do more public relations, approach appropriate clubs and churches for help, ask present volunteers to become recruiters, etc.

If turnover were the problem, alternatives might be to evaluate the entire program (involving volunteers, staff and clients to decide what changes are needed); provide better in-service training; cut down the number of jobs open to volunteers; or present in-service training for staff on the effective use of volunteers.

In both instances, the alternatives could be to implement one of the suggestions, all of them—or do nothing at all. The desired process would be to decide on the best one or more actions, set priorities for them and then to act on them.

One other comment before we leave decision-making. As a general rule, decisions should be made as far down on the organization scale as possible, and include those people whom the decision affects. In this case, volunteers, staff and clients should be involved in the process, since the decision will affect them all.

We have just considered five habits of effective managers. Now let us examine *the actual functions of a manager*. There are various opinions among management theorists as to how to list these. The most commonly accepted are: 1) *planning,* 2) *organizing,* 3) *staffing,* 4) *directing* and 5) *controlling.*[7]

Let us examine each of these functions briefly and see what relevance they may have for volunteer programs.

1. *Planning.* This is the most basic of the management functions and it undergirds the other four functions. Without it we become like the man who was lost on a Los Angeles freeway, but assured his wife she had nothing to worry about because they were making such good time. Planning is fundamentally choosing a course of action from among alternative ways of doing something. It bridges the gap between where we are now and where we want to go. In other words, it is determining *what* has to be done.

    One of the more popular and widely used concepts in the area of planning the past several years has been *Management by Objectives.* In its simplest form MBO is determining *who* is going to do *what, when* and *how.*

    While recognizing the importance of setting objectives, we would be remiss not to mention the importance of remaining flexible and open to change. Perhaps we could use the analogy of a football team to illustrate. Although a team's objective is to win a game, plans usually have to be constantly altered to achieve this objective. For example, if the star quarterback is injured, the opposing team uses new and unexpected strategies, or a rainstorm suddenly changes the condition of the field, plans must be adjusted accordingly. The team that can best shift with changing realities and still move forward toward the objective will likely be the victor. It is the team that either has no well defined plan or holds rigidly to one when conditions change that is usually in trouble.

In our community, I have witnessed many voluntary efforts that have been launched with a cause, but not a plan. People observe a need and decide to do something about it. But all too frequently, the basic problems of researching existing services, funding, staffing, community education and support have not been dealt with and the effort flourishes for a few weeks and fades. Volunteers have been disillusioned and discouraged and clients have had their hopes raised for a time and then feel more despair than before. Plans must be carefully developed *before* programs are launched.

We will be discussing the process of planning in detail in Chapter V.

2. *Organizing*. This is how a manager groups and assigns activities that are needed to accomplish goals and objectives. It is simply determining *how* the job will be done.

Two essential ingredients involved in organizing are *delegation* and *coordination*.

Delegation is perhaps one of the most difficult management concepts for many Directors of Volunteers to implement and yet it is absolutely vital that it be done, and done well.

At the national conferences we have conducted at the University of Colorado for managers of volunteer programs, I have had countless personal consultations with Directors who have felt desperately over-worked, under-staffed, and under-funded. They reach a point of personal frustration when they spend a week at a conference learning of still more things they ought to be doing to have sound and successful volunteer programs, when they have too much to do already.

Normally, in these conversations it becomes apparent that many Directors feel a strong need to be the "doer" of most of the significant things that are done in their programs. It is at this point I feel compelled to confront them about their attitudes toward volunteers. Do they only believe in using volunteers with other people, other departments and other programs, or do they believe in them enough that they can begin to use them creatively and effectively themselves? I ask them to ask themselves these questions:

1) Do I have enough confidence in myself that I will not only accept, but actively seek out volunteers who know more than I do about a program area where I need help?

31

2) Am I willing to delegate *significant* parts of my program to qualified volunteers (and be glad, not threatened, if they succeed)?

3) Do the jobs I offer to high level volunteers within my program make a sensible, logical whole, or are they bits and pieces of busy work that give the volunteer little opportunity for satisfaction or growth?

4) Am I willing to shift from being a "doer" to being an "enabler"? In other words, can I become a good manager and find satisfaction in that?

I understand the frustrations of these people, because I have shared them for almost 7 years. Our Volunteer and Information Center has experienced tremendous growth during these years· (placing close to 5,000 volunteers in the 80 different community agencies we serve, and handling 12,000 information and referral calls as well). Our paid staff consists of myself and an Administrative Secretary (plus a staff of four who work only with our Retired Senior Volunteer Program). In order to respond to the constantly increasing demands on our services, we decided very early that paid staff alone was not the answer, nor would it ever be. If we were to espouse volunteerism in our community it seemed only appropriate that we demonstrate we could make it work ourselves.

The single most helpful thing to me, as Director, in facing the issue of delegation was, and still is, being very honest and realistic about my own limitations, both of time and knowledge. Once I had dealt with that issue, it became not only desireable, but clearly essential that I bring in capable, knowledgeable volunteers to help. We now have high level volunteers in charge of eleven well defined and essential Task Forces (although they could be called Committees, Task Groups, etc.). Some of these are: Youth Recruitment; Senior Citizen Involvement (RSVP); School Aide and Tutor Program; "Do Something" Council (Group Projects); Research; Office Assistants; Public Relations.

This method of delegation is just as appropriate for a Director of Volunteers within a large agency. The jobs or Task Forces defined would vary, depending on the thrust, needs and size of each program, but the concept is workable, as long as the Director is willing to delegate. I have found having volunteers in these responsible positions to be not only workable, but exceedingly valuable. They bring fresh ideas, vigor and dedication that surpasses many paid staffs I have seen.

Some examples of these types of assignments in other agencies might be:

MENTAL HEALTH CLINIC:

Office Volunteers	Recruitment	Training	Public Relations	Transportation

COURTS AND CORRECTIONS:

Recruitment	Testing	Tutoring Program	Vol. Probation	Jail Visitation

DAY CARE CENTER:

Office Volunteers	Playground Volunteers	Equipment & Grounds	Visiting Resource Program	Arts & Crafts

The key is to find one knowledgeable and competent volunteer to be in charge of each of these areas—then delegate responsibility for that program area to him or her. They in turn delegate to other volunteers in that program. This then is the pyramid effect:

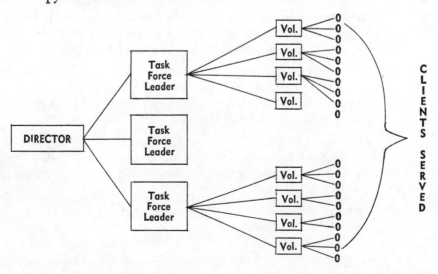

The most important factors I have found useful in helping me to delegate effectively are these:

1) *To define clearly and creatively the responsibilities being delegated to each person,* being sure agreement is reached as to areas in which this person can function freely and where the limits are.

2) *To delegate segments that make sense and not bits and pieces.*

   For example: Our Youth Task Force leader is responsible for the recruitment, interviewing, placing and follow-up of all teenage volunteers. He or she is free to design materials, slide shows, and brochures (checking with me regarding budgetary implications) and conduct any type of recruitment appropriate for teens. The teen volunteer program is their responsibility.

3) *To choose appropriate people for the assignment* by interviewing and placing paid and volunteer staff carefully, maximizing strengths and minimizing weaknesses. *Seeking out* skills and knowledge needed.

4) *To mutually set goals and standards of performance.* Expectations must be clearly defined. (*Do not* lower standards for volunteer staff, as it is an insult to a good volunteer.)

5) *To give accurate and honest feedback.* People want to know how they are doing and they deserve to know. This is both an opportunity for giving satisfaction and for encouraging growth. Allow risk-taking and mistakes.

6) *To support co-workers—both paid and volunteer by sharing knowledge, information, and plans with them.* It is incredible how many errors are made simply because of a lack of information. (Share their failures as well as successes.)

7) *To, whenever possible, give those who are responsible for carrying out significant portions of the program a voice in the decision-making body.* In other words, put them on the Board or Advisory Committee.

8) *To really delegate!* Most responsible people, when given a project, do not appreciate someone looking over their shoulder, kibitzing by phone or taking back parts of the assignment before they have had a chance to do it. Many

managers find it extremely difficult to really let go. Once again they want to be the doers. This is critical to successful delegation. This only works if the previous suggestions are followed, i.e., mutually set goals, staff support, etc. Delegation does not mean throwing someone out there to sink or swim on their own. It means enabling someone to do the job you've asked them to do.

These same basic principles apply for any kind of delegation. For example, a social worker should clearly define the responsibilities she or he is delegating to a volunteer big brother of a client (after carefully interviewing him for the assignment). The paid person must take the time and care with that volunteer to mutually set goals and expectations of what is to be achieved, give *regular* and honest feedback to him, and professional back-up and support as needed, accept his feedback and concerns and *trust him* to do a good job of being a friend to the client.

What delegation does not do is eliminate work, it simply changes it. As a person is able to delegate appropriately, you see a multiplier effect occur. The time spent doing one job can be spent in enabling several people to do numerous jobs.

But management is hard work and at times it may seem easier just to do it yourself. I know I feel that way at times. But then I have a mental picture of my situation which helps me gain perspective again. I envision myself sitting on top of the famous Budweiser wagon. The beautiful Clydesdales charging out in front of the wagon are my Task Force leaders. I feel both exhilarated and a bit overwhelmed by their force and tremendous energy, especially knowing that I have only two thin reins to guide them and to see that we are all going where we need to go. At times, especially when several leaders come in with new ideas at the same time, I am sorely tempted to cut those reins and let them all go. But then I realize my only alternative would be to climb down from the wagon and try to pick it up and move it myself. It is absolutely clear to me I would be unable to go anywhere at all. (It is amazing how appealing delegation looks after this little exercise.)

Coordination is the essential function of making certain that the right hand knows what the left hand is doing or that the volunteers know what staff is doing and vice versa. This is vital to ensure that each segment of the program is congruent

35

with the whole and that every opportunity for cooperation between people and between programs is encouraged and developed to the fullest. It is astounding how much wasted effort is caused by lack of coordination within an agency or between agencies. This is a responsibility that we, as managers, must recognize and fulfill more effectively.

Let us examine a few examples of lack of coordination in volunteer programs:

—A psychiatric social worker decides to change the method or goal of treatment for a patient (i.e., behavior modification). However, he fails to inform the volunteer who works with this patient 2 to 4 hours a week and they end up working at cross-purposes with the patient (who decides to play one against the other) due to lack of coordination and communication.

—A youth agency received a large grant for a new inner-city program. Most of the paid staff and volunteers were not informed of this, nor were they involved in the planning. They read about it in the newspaper and were embarrassed and defensive as friends and other agency people asked them about it, as they were totally uninformed. No exploration had been done to see how existing volunteer services, public relations and other staff could assist in this new program, but rather duplicate services were established in the new offices. Resentment and frustration were almost inevitable as staff and volunteers from both programs began to compete rather than coordinate their efforts.

—Agency X is a nursing home which uses volunteers—as does Agency Y (also a nursing home four blocks away). Agency X decided to invite a state expert on nursing home volunteer programs to present an orientation for their paid staff and volunteers. Not until the event was over did it occur to the Director of Volunteers that Agency Y might have appreciated being invited to share in this training event (and possibly even the expenses incurred).

In Chapter IX we will discuss the problems of communication which is the key to coordination. In these three cases the problems could have been avoided by:

1) regularly scheduled meetings between the staff person and his volunteers;

2) new program ideas being shared with total staff and their input being incorporated from the beginning;

3) a simple phone call from one Director to another.

Rensis Likert, in his book *New Patterns of Management* describes another important aspect of coordination and he calls this the "linking pin concept." He states, "The capacity to exert influence upward is essential if a supervisor [or manager] is to perform his supervisory functions successfully."[8] This means a manager needs to serve as the group's representative at higher levels in the organization and heirarchy, and be involved in long-range planning, interdepartmental coordination and acquisition of resources.

3. *Staffing.* This is determining *who* is going to do the job. In volunteer programs, this includes volunteers as well as paid staff. Managers must recruit, select, train, promote and discharge paid and non-paid staff. Since later Chapters will be dealing with all of these topics, we will move on to the next function.

4. *Directing.* This refers to getting people (or in many cases, allowing them) to accomplish the tasks assigned to them. In other words it is getting the work done. All the planning in the world is in vain unless the plans are implemented. This involves motivating, communicating with and leading staff.

> *Motivating*—in Chapter III we deal with this at length. It is simply understanding the "whys" of behavior as they relate to each person who works for you. Knowing what motivates your people is difficult to determine, but it is something the successful manager must do.

> *Communicating*—in Chapter IX we will discuss the complex communications challenge to the Director of Volunteers. This includes communicating with (and listening to) volunteers, staff, administration, clients and the community. Many times the job is not done well because we were inaccurate or incomplete in our giving and receiving of information and assignments.

> *Leading*—note this does not say pushing, pulling or coercing people—but leading them.

How a person leads or manages others reflects his or her most basic assumptions about people. In Chapter IV we will explore various leadership styles and the tremendous impact this has on the climate of the organization and the motivation of the people who work there.

Harriet Naylor addresses this issue in her book, *Volunteers Today*, when she states, "A new style of leadership is demanded. A dynamic, eclectic approach with courage to experiment, to weed out the useless and yet to hold fast to ideals, standards and essential values. Such leaders do not develop by being told what to do. Rather, they respond to our faith in them and in their capacity to learn and do. They need active learning opportunities, to try new knowledge and discover how to make it work for them in their own situations, tapping their own resources."[9]

5. *Controlling.* This is the process of evaluation which is essential if the manager is to determine if events have conformed to plans. In other words, did we get lost on the freeway or get where we were going? This enables us to make sure plans are carried out and objectives accomplished—and if they are not, we will be able to determine why—and what we need to do about it (alter plans, change staff, change procedures, etc.).

Evaluation, the chief tool of control, is frequently overlooked by many volunteer programs because we get so involved in the doing. However, if we are to have quality programs it is essential. It is possible and even desireable to have both formal and informal evaluations.

The formal might consist of questionnaires sent to staff, volunteers and clients asking specific questions about the quality, value, strengths and weaknesses of the program. Or it could consist of periodic personal or telephone interviews with random samples of each of the above groups.

Informal evaluations should go on constantly. It occurs over coffee, in elevators, in the hall and on the job. It is both seeing and hearing how things are going and being sensitively atuned to potential problems before they occur.

Summary: Perhaps it would be helpful to translate these management functions into the terminology of volunteer administration:

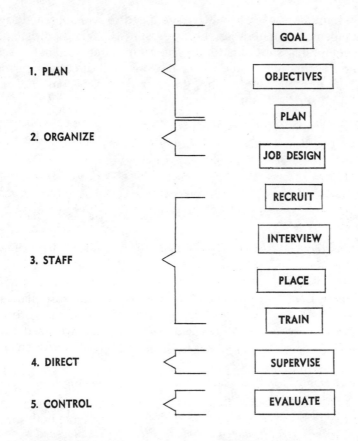

1. PLAN — GOAL, OBJECTIVES, PLAN

2. ORGANIZE — PLAN, JOB DESIGN

3. STAFF — RECRUIT, INTERVIEW, PLACE, TRAIN

4. DIRECT — SUPERVISE

5. CONTROL — EVALUATE

Hopefully the relevancy becomes apparent. By following this logical sequence of sound management practice, the probability of having well organized and productive volunteer programs is greatly increased. It is how we can avoid such problems as recruiting volunteers before needs and jobs have been defined; placing volunteers inappropriately due to failing to interview; or repeating past mistakes by never evaluating programs.

In conclusion, let us once again examine if and why we in human service organizations need to be concerned about management. According to Peter Drucker, in his book entitled *Management: Tasks, Responsibilities, Practices,* which was published in 1974, management is a growing concern in nonbusiness institutions simply because it has been a glaring weakness in the past. He claims that managing service institutions and agencies is probably going to be the frontier of managment for the rest of this century.[10]

When moving from "if" to "why" we need to be concerned about our management capabilities, Drucker states, "Whether the manager develops his subordinates in the right direction, helps them grow and become bigger and richer persons, will directly determine whether he himself will develop, grow or wither, become richer or become impoverished, improved or deteriorate."[11]

Perhaps that is why the ancient oriental sage, Lao-Tzu, observed, "When the best leader's work is done, the people say. 'We did it ourselves'."

References

1. Drucker, Peter F., *The Practice of Management*, Harper & Bros., 1954, p. 6.

2. Townsend, Robert, *Up the Organization*, Alfred A. Knopf, Inc., 1970, p. 26.

3. Ibid, p. 116.

4. McGregor, Douglas, *The Human Side of Enterprise*, McGraw-Hill, 1960, pp. 28 and 29.

5. Quoted in Townsend, *Up the Organization*, p. 81.

6. Drucker, Peter F., *The Effective Executive*, Harper & Row, 1966. p. 23 ff.

7. Koontz, Harold and O'Donnell, Cyril, *Principles of Management*, McGraw-Hill, 1955-1968. p. 48-50.

8. Likert, Rensis, *New Patterns of Management*, McGraw-Hill, 1961, p. 14.

9. Naylor, Harriet H., *Volunteers Today: Finding, Training and Working With Them*, Dryden Assoc., 1967 & 73, pp. 18 and 19.

10. Drucker, Peter F., *Management: Tasks, Responsibilities, Practices*, Harper & Row, 1973-74, pp. 8 and 9.

11. Drucker, *Practice of Management*, p. 348.

CHAPTER III

Motivation: The Whys of Behavior

"Citizens you are all brothers, yet God has framed you different-ly." These sage words of Plato may perhaps help to explain why a 50-year old friend of mine has just taken a class in belly-dancing, while a 30-year old neighbor has decided to learn the art of quilting.

One of the delightful things about life is that people are different, not just in physical appearance, but in abilities, emotional makeup, cultural heritage and in what they do and do not like to do.

It is fascinating to contemplate the "whys" of behavior. Why do people choose skiing instead of butterfly catching, reading rather than bridge, or auto mechanics instead of medicine? Or why does one volunteer prefer to work with delinquent youngsters and an-other enjoy routine office tasks?

Since management is simply working with and through individuals and groups to accomplish organizational goals, it would seem evi-dent that one priority for managers would be to understand as much as possible about why people do things (or do not do them).

There are very good reasons why so many idealistic, worthwhile social programs fail. Two such reasons, I believe, are a lack of knowl-

41

edge of management and organizational skills and secondly, a naive and oversimplified view of people and motivation. Knowing what we want our organizations to do is relatively easy. Knowing how to make it happen is something else. As Yeats once observed "In dreams begin responsibilities".

In *Organizational Behavior and the Practice of Management* Hampton, Summer, and Webber state, "Behavior on the job is a function of what the person brings to the situation and what the situation brings to the person. When people come to work in organizations they do not come 'empty handed' . . . they bring various needs or motives which predispose them to release their energy or behave in particular ways—ways which seem to them likely to satisfy their needs".[1]

The authors depict motivation as being like a scissor. One blade is what a person brings to a situation (or job) and the other blade is what the situation brings to the person. "It is only as the blades come together that the pattern of behavior is cut."[2]

Obviously we must look at both factors if we are really going to understand why a person does what he does. Let's begin with the first blade—what a person brings to the job.

Since human beings are extremely intricate and complex organisms, any attempt to simplistically diagnose "why I am like I am", or "why I do what I do" would be impossible within the limits of one chapter of one small book. What we can do is summarize for you some of the better known theories of motivation and then see what practical applications they may have for managing a volunteer program.

One of the first things we must be aware of is the necessity to distinguish between a person's *ability* to do something and his *will* to do it. A volunteer might be perfectly able to perform a task (he or she has the necessary skills and knowledge to stuff envelopes or give a speech), but they simply do not want to do it. In other words, they lack the motivation for that particular assignment. Or, a volunteer may want very much to edit a newsletter, but lacks the skill and training to do so.

Sometimes it is easy to equate our need for a particular skill with a person's willingness to perform it, without ever bothering to check out that assumption with the person. An example would be, when our Volunteer & Information Center receives 150-200 requests for volunteer aides and tutors for elementary schools each fall, it is

42

amazing how easily we can convince ourselves that every volunteer who walks into our office for several weeks is eager to work with children, and especially within the school system. Our need has a tendency to create filters which hinder us from hearing the volunteers' needs and interests.

Let us turn then, to the behavioral scientists to see what they can tell us about motivation that might help us with the down-to-earth problems and challenges of managing a program. Perhaps it will give us new insight into such things as absenteeism, turnover, attitude and performance as it relates to both our paid staff and volunteers.

Undoubtedly one of the most well-known theories is that of Abraham Maslow, a former president of the American Psychological Association. His "hierarchy of needs" has become a classic and is studied in psychology and behavorial science classes everywhere. He got the unique idea that we could learn as much about people by studying healthy, well-adjusted people as we could by studying those with problems, so that is what he did. His conclusion was that each of us has various levels of need and as we satisfy one need level, we move up to the next. These needs he categorized as follows:

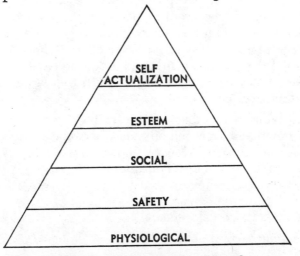

Figure 1: Maslow's Hierarchy of Needs[3]

Physiological—the basic physical needs for food, water, air, sex, etc.
Safety—the need to be safe from harm, to have security.
Social—the need for affiliation or closeness with others; to be liked.
Esteem—the need to be recognized as a person of value; to be rewarded.
Self-Actualization—the highest need, which Maslow called life's "peak experience." (Freud referred to this as the "ego ideal.") This means a person will not be ultimately happy unless he is doing what he is fitted for . . . "A musician must make music, an artist paint, a poet write . . . what a man *can* be, he *must* be."[4]

43

Two interesting observations Maslow made were: 1) *Man is a "wanting creature"* and as soon as one level of need is satisfied, we move on to the next (or if a basic need is suddenly not met, such as not having food or safety, all other needs become unimportant, and we regress on the hierarchy); and 2) *a met need is no longer a motivator.*

When we remember that what a person needs is what will motivate him, then we begin to see the significance this has regarding a person's performance on the job, whether that job is paid or unpaid. Does this also suggest some interesting possibilities about why people volunteer in the first place? Or choose not to volunteer at all?

The second theory we will examine is Frederick Herzberg's "Motivation-Hygiene theory".[6] Herzberg separates factors affecting people (and how they work) into two categories: *hygiene factors* and *motivators.*

He categorizes things that relate to a person's work environment as *hygiene factors.* These include policies, administration, supervision, working conditions, interpersonal relations, status, security and money. He made the interesting observation that these things in themselves do not motivate people, but *the absence of them demotivates them.* In other words, a pleasant work area or new insurance plan will not motivate people to do more or better work, but if they are not present, they can have a negative effect on a person's motivation. Likewise, a new title and a desk to sit at will not cause a volunteer to stay or do better work but if they are missing, they may affect his morale.

The satisfying factors that involve feelings of achievement, professional growth, and recognition that a person can experience in a job that offers challenge and scope, Herzberg refers to as *motivators.* They relate to the job itself and include:

—*achievement*

—*recognition for accomplishment*

—*challenging work*

—*increased responsibility*

—*growth and development*

At a recent workshop of over 70 Directors of volunteer programs, we asked the participants to describe their most "turned on" volunteers. It was interesting to note that in each case one or more of

Herzberg's motivators were very clearly present. Some examples were:

—a volunteer who designed a raised map of a neighborhood area to help blind persons be able to travel unaided in the area (challenging work; achievement);

—the mother of a diabetic child who assisted a team of doctors, nurses and school staff in designing an educational brochure for schools to interpret the needs of diabetic children (recognition, challenging work, responsibility);

—the volunteer coach who worked four years with a youngsters' basketball team and developed the team so it won a dozen or more tournaments (achievement, recognition, work itself);

—a volunteer (in my own agency) who completely designed, researched and published the first Community Resource Directory for this county (achievement, challenge, responsibility and recognition).

If we fit the Maslow & Herzberg theories together, they overlay as follows:[5]

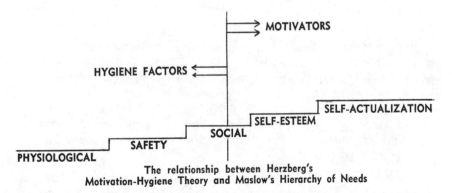

The relationship between Herzberg's
Motivation-Hygiene Theory and Maslow's Hierarchy of Needs

Later in this Chapter we will examine these theories again and make an effort to apply them to our specific areas of concern. But before we do this, let us look at another approach to understanding motivation.

In a book entitled *Motivation and Organizational Climate,* the work of researchers David C. McClelland and John W. Atkinson is presented. They identified three distinct motives which affect people's work-related behavior:[6]

1. The need for achievement;
2. The need for power; and
3. The need for affiliation.

They point out that motives start in the head, for our thoughts determine how we talk and act. In other words, how we think determines how we act.

Let's use our imaginations a moment and utilizing the research of Atkinson and McClelland visualize a huge reservoir of energy (and we'll call that reservoir *motivation*). Then we'll draw three valves, or openings, in the reservoir through which energy flows, and those we'll label *power, achievement* and *affiliation*.

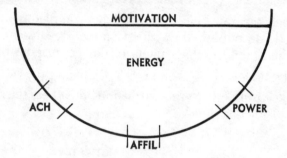

Each motive (or flow through each valve) leads to a different kind of behavior. People have all three valves or motives, but they vary as to size and how much they are used. We might say—

—*STRONG MOTIVE*—A valve or energy outlet that opens easily, and is larger so more energy can flow through (usually because it's used more). This will determine the type of behavior engaged in by this person.

—*WEAK MOTIVE*—A tight, or sticky valve that allows only a tiny bit of energy through (almost like it's rusted shut). Again this influences types of action or responses on the part of any individual.

McClelland and Atkinson found that the presence and strength of these motives in a person can actually be tested through what is called *Thematic Apperception Methods* (TAT). You are simply shown a set of pictures depicting various social and work situations and are asked to write imaginative stories about them. What happens is that you project your thoughts, feelings and attitudes into the stories and they provide a sample of what you spend your time thinking and dreaming about. And remember—*how you think determines how you act*, so this becomes a relatively accurate predictor of behavior.

Obviously we can not all take *TATS* or give them to our fellow employees or volunteers, but we can do the next best thing. By looking at some of the characteristics and behavior patterns that McClelland and Atkinson have identified with each of the three motives, we can become better able to determine the needs our volunteers and employees bring to the job. Hopefully we can in turn create jobs and climates that better meet those needs.[7]

A. *ACHIEVEMENT MOTIVATED PERSON*

Goal: Success in a situation which requires excellent or improved performance.

Characteristics:
   —Concern with excellence and wanting to do personal best; sets moderate goals and takes calculated risks;
   —Likes to take personal responsibility for finding solutions to problems;
   —Has desire to achieve unique accomplishments;
   —Restless and innovative—takes pleasure in striving;
   —Wants concrete feedback.

Spends Time Thinking About:
   —Doing job better;
   —Accomplishing something unsual or important;
   —Advancing his career;
   —Goals and how he can attain them *and* obstacles and how he can overcome them.

   (To illustrate—Sir Isaac Newton was once asked how he ever discovered gravity and he matter-of-factly replied, "By thinking about it all the time!")

B. *POWER MOTIVATED PERSON*

Goal: Having impact or influence on others.

Characteristics:
   —Concern for reputation or position (and what people think of his power and influence);
   —Gives advice (sometimes unsolicited);

—Wants his ideas to predominate (like Archie Bunker when he said "It's times like this, Edith, where the only thing holding a marriage together is the husband being big enough to step back and see where his wife is wrong");
—Strong feelings about status and prestige;
—Strong need to influence others; to change other people's behavior;
—Often verbally fluent (sometimes argumentative);
—Seen by others as forceful, outspoken and even hard-headed.

Spends Time Thinking About:
—Influence and control he has over others;
—How he can use this influence to win arguments, change people, gain status and authority.

McClelland, however, in an article published in the Journal of International Affairs in 1970, entitled, *"Two Faces of Power"* points out some mistaken notions we have in this country concerning the need for power. He states we have almost totally overlooked the fact that power has two "faces"—one negative and one positive. We tend to assume any leader with power must have dominated the group and attained his power at the expense of the others. This is sometimes true, but not always.

He identifies the negative type of power as *personalized power* and the positive he calls *socialized power*. He characterizes each as follows:[8]

PERSONALIZED (Negative)	SOCIALIZED (Positive)
I win—you lose	I win—you win
Law of the jungle	Exercises power for benefit of others to attain group goals
Prestige supplies (i.e., biggest desk, nicest office, newest car)	Charismatically inspires others to action
Personal power and authority —autocrat	Creates confidence in others— helps them achieve group goals
Makes group dependent and submissive	Makes people feel like origins, not pawns
Exerts personal dominance	
Tends to treat people like pawns, not origins	

48

He cautions that if our society insists on overlooking or disregarding the positive use of power, we will continue to see our young people shun public office and positions of leadership. It would seem evident that we must start to reinforce the positive face of power, or in the future we will have even more difficulty getting good volunteers to run for school boards, city councils, university regents, city and county planning boards. Like so many other things, power is not bad in and of itself, it is the misuse of it that is.

C. AFFILIATION MOTIVATED PERSON

Goal: Being with someone else and enjoying mutual friendship.

Characteristics:
—Concerned with being liked and accepted—inter-personal relationships;
—Needs warm and friendly relationships and interaction;
—Concerned about being separated from other people (definitely not the loner).

Spends Time Thinking About:
—Wanting to be liked and how to achieve this;
—Consoling or helping people;
—Warm and friendly relationships;
—The feelings of others and himself.

The administrative implications of McClelland's and Atkinson's motivation theory we have just described are quite dramatic:

1. *Managers can select people* whose motivational drive fits the job to be done;
2. Or vice-versa—we can *fit the job to the motivational needs of the worker;*
3. *Managers can do things to work situation* or organization which will help get the job done; and
4. We, as managers, *can change ourselves* relative to how we lead others.

There is one final theory that we will examine briefly, because it is currently viewed with great interest by contemporary psychologists and industrial sociologists as it relates to organizational behavior. This theory is called the "expectancy theory." In its simplest form, the expectancy theory sees the anticipation of a reward (or desired outcome) as functioning selectively on actions expected to lead to it.

V. H. Vroom seems to be a leader in this particular school of thought. He defines motivation as a "process governing choices among forms of voluntary activity"; and, expectancy as "a belief concerning the likelihood that a particular act will be followed by a particular outcome".[9] His motivation model explains how goals influence efforts.

He identifies two levels of outcomes. How a person acts regarding first level outcome is greatly influenced by the strength of his desire for a particular second level outcome.

In an organizational setting, some first class outcomes might be such things as money, promotion, recognition, etc. However, Vroom suggests these may have little value by themselves, but are valuable because they enable a person to secure second level outcomes such as food, clothing, travel, status, etc. If the second level goal is important enough, it encourages the actions (such as high performance, dependability) that would accomplish the first level outcome (promotion).

According to J. G. Hunt and J. W. Hill in an article entitled *"The New Look in Motivation Theory for Organizational Theory,"* Vroom's motivational model holds great promise in predicting behavior in organizations. However, more research is definitely needed to deal with the many questions as yet unanswered.

A word specifically about the motivation of volunteers might be in order here.

In ACTION's report entitled *Americans Volunteer—1974,* the Census Bureau survey reported the following data concerning people's reasons for volunteering.[10] (Note: they could check more than one, therefore percentages total more than 100%.) The answers are correlated with a similar survey conducted in 1965.

Reasons	1965	1974
Wanted to help others	37%	53%
Had sense of duty	33%	32%
Enjoy volunteer work itself	30%	36%
Could not refuse	6%	15%
Had child in program	22%	22%
Had nothing else to do	4%	4%
Hoped would lead to paying job	3%	3%
Other	7%	7%

When asked if they planned to do volunteer work next year, the 3 most popular categories for positive responses (each showing 6% increase or more) were: helping others, enjoying volunteer work and sense of duty. All other options showed a slight decline.

Because of the high percentage who noted the extreme importance of the job the agency asked them to do, and how they felt this benefited them personally, I think it behooves us to give considerable thought and care to the business of defining our volunteer jobs. We will deal with this in Chapter VI.

This probably all adds up to a verification of the old saw "different strokes for different folks." The challenge comes in being sensitive enough to recognize which strokes mean something to a particular volunteer or staff person so we are speaking to their needs and not just our own. (Of course, recognizing their needs without doing anything about it is almost worse than being insensitive to them in the first place.)

The rest of this book will address itself to how we as managers of volunteer programs can utilize an understanding of motivation in all aspects of our programs. However, I would like to make a few very specific observations at this point.

VOLUNTEER JOB DESIGN. It would seem that most of the more basic needs on Maslow's hierarchy have been met in the majority of people who have time and energy to volunteer. We must therefore rethink the jobs we are offering them to be sure they are generously laced with motivators and not overly encumbered with hygiene factors. Do the jobs allow the volunteer opportunities for developing new skills, gaining self awareness and self-esteem, and hopefully, for those few who are ready, the chance *to become,* or to self-actualize? Or are our job boxes so carefully carved and religiously guarded that a person fits into one of those boxes or feels forced to move on?

It has been found by industry that the best motivator to keep people on the job is the work itself. This is certainly true of volunteers as well.

So ask yourself—are my volunteer jobs interesting and challenging enough to hold people in them? Then ask the volunteers who are doing the jobs and listen carefully to what they suggest. Finally, together re-think that position and see if there are ways it might be enlarged or enriched, and most importantly, made more fun! (Staff and clients should be included in this as well.)

You might find your volunteer recruiters have some very valid and exciting ideas about your brochure, slide shows and interviewing procedures that would make the job easier, and your program more effective. But nobody ever asked their opinion and besides the job description states they give presentations (not design them). Getting good volunteers is the task of recruitment—keeping them is everybody's job.

RECRUITING VOLUNTEERS. The most frequent mistake in recruitment is to look in the wrong places for the right people. Once your jobs have been defined, brainstorm with the staff and volunteers to determine where you are most apt to find the skills you need. Recruiting for envelope stuffers and stamp lickers at the University Faculty Wives Club does not make very good business sense. Or speaking to a service club where members are all working professional people about becoming day-care aides is self-defeating. They want to help, but they work the same hours the day care center is open. Determining what skills you need is important, but equally crucial is considering "What are the needs and motives of the people I am trying to recruit?" Offer the right person a meaningful job to do that is appropriate for their personal goals and realities and recruitment is a cinch. For example, Home Extension Clubs would very likely have volunteers who would like to help start a nutrition program for the elderly; Future Teachers' groups at a high school are likely recruiting grounds for tutors for elementary schools; and, an Artists' Guild would probably be a good place to seek out judges for a youngsters' art contest.

Another issue Maslow's theory may shed some light on is the difficulty almost all volunteer programs are having in recruiting minority and low income volunteers. Perhaps what Maslow is telling us is they have more crucial and personal needs that need attention, such as having enough food or safe and adequate housing and that rightfully so—these take precedence over our needs at this moment. If we as a society can help them meet their basic needs, then perhaps we have a right to ask them to help us meet our needs and the needs of our clients. It's an interesting and challenging thought. More about this in Chapter VI.

INTERVIEWING AND PLACING VOLUNTEERS. Since we will be spending an entire Chapter on this subject I simply want to suggest at this point that the interview is the first and probably best place to determine a volunteer's needs and goals. How long has it been since you purposefully asked a potential volunteer such questions as "What do you hope to gain from this volunteer experience?" "What sort of things do you most like to do and why?" or "Describe what you dislike in a job." One way to determine what strokes are important to this person is to ask him or her. Just the knowledge that you care enough to ask may offer incentive enough for that volunteer to want to work with you.

McClelland's research gives us much to think about regarding the placing of volunteers in appropriate positions. Do we have achievers in jobs that do not allow for innovation or unique accomplishments? Are affiliation motivated volunteers working by themselves? Are power motivated volunteers in jobs where they only take orders and never have an opportunity to direct or influence others?

SUPERVISION. The manager who manages everyone alike is in deep trouble. Once again he is saying, in essence, "I know what my personal and organizational needs are . . . but I don't really know or care what yours are". A volunteer who works in a routine, sporadic assignment has very little in common (as far as type of supervision that is appropriate) with the deeply committed volunteer in a highly responsible job. Also, depending on whether the person is achievement, power or affiliation motivated, your supervisory style needs to vary with individuals.

For example, achievement oriented persons usually respond best to well-delegated, clearly articulated assignments. The manager needs to be direct, business-like and trusting enough of these persons not to be constantly checking up or making decisions for them. The manager's role is one of mentor, advisor and supporter.

The power motivated volunteer or staff worker needs clear cut policy and procedural frameworks within which to operate. The manager needs to portray a stronger authority image with this person, for they need and want it. Informality and indecisiveness are often upsetting. They want to know "the rules of the game", so they can play it well—and hopefully become a leader of part of the team someday. The manager's role is one of leader.

Affiliation motivated people need a leader/friend. The manager who is all business both frightens and alienates this type of person. They are sensitive and easily hurt, so the climate must be accepting, supportive and genuinely friendly. They are eager to invest their loyalty in a leader who cares about them and what they do.

The important thing is to be the enabler that helps each person realize his or her own full potential. As a Chinese sage, Lao-Tzu observed, "To lead people, walk behind them."

RECOGNITION/REWARD. This subject is very closely associated with motivation. If we reward people with things that are not significant to them, then the whole process is wasted. There are volunteers who find pins, certificates and luncheons truly meaningful and the recognition and self-esteem involved speaks to their own level of need. The difficulty has arisen when we as Directors have assumed that these were appropriate and significant for all volunteers.

There are some achievement oriented people who will honestly tell you that the most meaningful recognition they can receive is more responsible and meaningful work . . . in other words, a promotion. To a power motivated individual, a new title or the opportunity to train or supervise other volunteers holds much more value than a pin or plaque.

Once again it is our responsibility to know which strokes for which folks.

TURNOVER. If people are leaving your organization, there are reasons and you must know what those are if you are to reverse the exodus. Maybe the phrases "met needs do not motivate" or "man is a wanting creature—when one level of need is met, he moves on to the next" are good bench marks for us. Also, it is helpful to examine why people stay with your program.

Are you designing *meaningful* jobs and supervising your volunteers in a way that not only allows for, but encourages personal growth? If not, the only thing that should surprise you is that you are surprised that there is turnover.

In conclusion, Harriet Naylor in her book, *Volunteers Today— Finding, Training and Working with Them*, states, "the feeling of being in tune with the whole is of prime importance to a volunteer on the job." She quotes the following summary on volunteer motivation by J. Donald Philips, President of Hillsdale College, Hillsdale, Michigan:[11]

"VOLUNTEER VIEWPOINT"

If you want my loyalty, interests and best efforts, remember that . . .

1. I need a SENSE OF BELONGING, a feeling that I am honestly needed for my total self, not just for my hands, nor because I take orders well.

2. I need to have a sense of sharing in planning our objectives. My need will be satisfied only when I feel that my ideas have had a fair hearing.

3. I need to feel that the goals and objectives arrived at are within reach and that they make sense to me.

4. I need to feel that what I'm doing has real purpose or contributes to human welfare—that its value extends even beyond my personal gain, or hours.

5. I need to share in making the rules by which, together, we shall live and work toward our goals.

6. I need to know in some clear detail just what is expected of me—not only my detailed task but where I have opportunity to make personal and final decisions.

7. I need to have some responsibilities that challenge, that are within range of my abilities and interest, and that contribute toward reaching my assigned goal, and that cover all goals.

8. I need to see that progress is being made toward the goals we have set.

9. I need to be kept informed. What I'm not up on, I may be down on. (Keeping me informed is one way to give me status as an individual.)

10. I need to have confidence in my superiors—confidence based upon assurance of consistent fair treatment, or recognition when it is due, and trust that loyalty will bring increased security.

In brief, it really doesn't matter how much sense my part in this organization makes to you—I must feel that the whole deal makes sense to me."

I would add, hopefully the whole deal makes sense to everyone involved—the client, staff, volunteer . . . and you.

References

1. Hampton, David R., Summer, Charles E., & Webber, Ross A., *Organizational Behavior and the Practice of Management,* Foresman & Co., 1973, p. 47.

2. Ibid, p. 47.

3. Hersey, Paul & Blanchard, Kenneth H., *Management of Organizational Behavior,* Prentice-Hall, Inc., 1972 (Second edition), p. 26.

4. Ibid, p. 23-24.

5. Ibid, p. 55.

6. Litwin, George H., and Stringer, Robert A., Jr., *Motivation and Organizational Climate,* Harvard Univ., 1968, p. 8.

7. Ibid, p. 14-24.

8. McClelland, David, "Two Faces of Power" quoted in Hampton, Summer & Webber, *Organizational Behavior and the Practice of Management.*

9. Hampton, Summer & Webber, p. 46.

10. *Americans Volunteer—1974,* a survey by the Census Bureau. ACTION, Office of Planning & Policy, Washington, D.C., 20525, 1974, p. 12-13.

11. Naylor, Harriet H., *Volunteers Today: Finding, Training and Working With Them,* Dryden Assoc., 1967-73, p. 66-67.

CHAPTER IV

Organizational Climate

The term "organizational climate" is used by behavioral scientists to describe how it feels to work in a particular situation or organization. You might say it is the atmosphere of any work community.

In the book *Motivation and Organizational Climate*, Litwin & Stringer define climate as "the perceived subjective effects of the formal system, the informal 'style' of managers, and other important environmental factors on attitudes, beliefs, values, and motivation of people who work in a particular organization".[1]

This concept is helpful in understanding, and hopefully dealing with the practical everyday problems of poor performance, lack of motivation, turnover, indifferent or hostile attitudes and conflicts between the personal goals of workers (whether paid or volunteer) and the goals of the agency or organization. It simply illustrates how environmental and interpersonal factors directly mold and shape both motivation and behavior. In other words, this is the second blade of the motivational scissor.

Litwin & Stringer point out that there are four distinct elements that affect work-related behavior:

1. The *motives and needs a person brings* to a situation;
2. *The job* or task to be done;
3. The personal strengths, weaknesses and *leadership style of the manager;* and
4. The *climate* of the organization.

We dealt with motivation in Chapter III, and will be discussing job design later in the book. Therefore we will pursue both leadership style and climate at this time, as they are very closely linked. In fact, research indicates that just as climate is one of the most important determinants of motivation, *managers are one of the major determinants of climate.* So our responsibility as managers would seem to be to understand climate and then to create effective, positive climates in our organizations.

Litwin and Stringer have identified nine dimensions or factors that determine and define climate. They are:[2]

1. *Structure*—the feeling that employees [and volunteers] have about the constraints in the group. How many rules, regulations, procedures are there; is there an emphasis on "red tape" and going through channels; or is there a loose and informal atmosphere?

2. *Responsibility*—the feeling of being your own boss; not having to double-check all your decisions. When you have a job to do, knowing that it is *your* job.

3. *Reward*—the feeling of being rewarded appropriately for a job well done; emphasizing positive rewards rather than punishments; the perceived fairness of the pay and promotion policies.

4. *Risk*—the sense of riskiness and challenge in the job and in the organization; is there an emphasis on taking calculated risks, or is playing it safe the best way to operate. [Does only paid staff get to take risks or are volunteers allowed that privilege?]

5. *Warmth*—the feeling of general good fellowship in the work group atmosphere; the emphasis on being well-liked; the prevalence of friendly and informal social groups. [The cooperation and good feeling between paid staff and volunteers and the absence of cliques.]

6. *Support*—the perceived helpfulness of the managers and others

in the group; emphasis on mutual support from above and below [and between staff and volunteers].

7. *Standards*—the perceived importance of implicit and explicit goals and performance standards; the emphasis on doing a good job; the challenge represented in personal and group goals. [Standards for volunteers set as high as staff.]

8. *Conflict*—the feeling that managers and other workers want to hear different opinions; the emphasis placed on getting problems out in the open, rather than smoothing them over or ignoring them.

9. *Identity*—the feeling that you belong to a group and you are a valuable member of a working team; the importance placed on this kind of spirit.

It is important to emphasize that these climate factors affect paid staffs and volunteers alike and should be viewed from both perspectives continuously. Also the client/consumer is greatly affected by the climate of the agency.

It would be tragic to recognize and deal with unhealthy climate problems for volunteers while perpetuating or ignoring them as they affect paid staff—or vice versa. As we said in the first paragraph, climate is how it feels to work in (and we might add, be served by) your organization.

And in volunteer programs perhaps the underlying factor that affects climate more than all of those stated by Litwin and Stringer is *trust*. It is implied in many of the other factors, but if it is missing, then it will have a tremendous impact on the whole organization. Trust must exist between volunteers, staff, clients, Director of volunteers and administration.

The authors go on to state that different climates stimulate different kinds of motivation, cause distinctive attitudes about a person's relationships with other workers and have a profound effect on both feelings of satisfaction and levels of performance.

Another interesting thing they discovered was that achievement motivation, affiliation motivation, and power motivation are aroused by very different kinds of climate.[3]

1. *To create an achievement-oriented climate they suggest*:

   a) emphasize personal responsibility;

   b) allow and encourage calculated risks and innovation; and

c) give recognition and reward for excellent performance—not for mediocre or poor performance.

2. *To create an affiliation-oriented climate*:
   a) encourage close, warm relationships;
   b) give considerable support and encouragement;
   c) provide a great deal of freedom and little structure or constraint; and
   d) make the individual feel like an accepted member of your group.

3. *To create a power-oriented climate*:
   a) provide considerable structure, such as rules, policies, etc.;
   b) allow people to obtain positions of responsibility, authority and status; and
   c) encourage the use of formal authority as a basis for resolving conflict and disagreement.

Although many things influence the climate of an organization (such as the past history of the organization, the type of organization, tasks to be done, and the needs and values of the group members), "the most important and dramatic determinant of climate seems to be the leadership style utilized by managers or by informal leaders."

In fact some researchers go one step further and state leadership determines not only climate, but the actual success or failure of many enterprises or organizations. They have determined that out of every 100 new business establishments started, almost half of them fail and go out of business within two years. By the end of five years only one-third of the original 100 are still in business and they maintain most of the failures can be attributed to ineffective leadership.[4]

If the rate of failure is that high in business, it is interesting to contemplate how high it would be in human service organizations if bureaucratic undergirdings, federal funding and traditional community support systems (e.g. United Way, local fund drives) were based more on productivity and effectiveness in meeting need and less on tradition, politics and grantsmanship. Perhaps we will soon know the answer, as the day of accountability seems to be upon us.

If leadership is so vitally important to the health and welfare of an organization, then it behooves us to spend some time examining it.

60

It would make our job delightfully simple if we could isolate the personal characteristics or traits of a good leader—whether they are tall or short, blue or brown-eyed, young or old, male or female, Protestant or Catholic, amiable or stern, etc. However, in fifty years of study, the experts have concluded that leadership is a dynamic process and varies from situation to situation, based on the unique combination of leader, follower, work to be done, and situation.

This suggests that we need to concentrate on the behavior of leaders, rather than leadership traits. The effective leader is the person who knows himself or herself, knows the people who work with him or her, and knows the situation, and is then able and willing to adapt leadership style to varying situations. Remember the point made earlier, that the manager does not have a role, but rather many roles to fill.

One of the most widely read and frequently quoted books on this subject is Douglas McGregor's *The Human Side of Enterprise*. McGregor maintained that how a leader leads (or manager manages) is based to a great extent on that person's basic assumptions about people. He identified two basic sets of assumptions clearly recognizable in work situations and called them Theory X and Theory Y.[5]

Theory X assumes that people are basically immature and irresponsible, that work is distasteful to them, that they want to be closely directed and controlled, and want to assume as little responsibility for their work as possible. A manager with this set of beliefs would tend to be very autocratic and authoritarian, making most decisions and exerting strong controls and close supervision.

Theory Y assumptions about people are very different. This theory believes people can and want to be basically self-directed and creative at work, that they are responsible and ambitious and that they want to develop their skills and abilities. The managers who makes these assumptions about workers tend to treat them as mature adults rather than children. They would tend to exert as little external control and supervision as possible in order to enable the worker to develop self-control and self-direction. These leaders attempt to unleash the potential that is within each person who works with them.

It would seem obvious that not all workers in any one situation fit either set of assumptions, nor that all leaders would be capable of acting exclusively in either one of the manners described. Once again, both followers and leaders are probably some combination of both. But McGregor clearly showed that our basic assumptions about people greatly affect how we treat most of the people much of the time and so has great significance for the manager, and in turn the climate of the organization.

These assumptions can be clearly observed in the very structuring of an organization. Theory "X" managers prefer vertical "top-down" systems, with the traditional hierarchical structure:

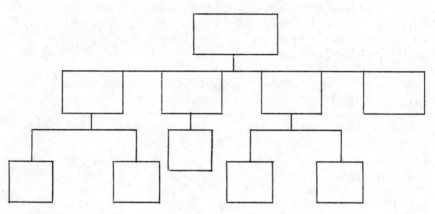

Whereas, Theory "Y" executives usually establish horizontal-participative systems:

More creative, high potential employees (and volunteers) are lost to organizations because of the stifling effects of Theory "X" bureaucracy than perhaps any other single reason.

And for Directors of Volunteers I think there is another significant point to consider. Are your assumptions about paid staff different than your assumptions about volunteers? In many organizations, it has appeared to me that there is a much greater tendency to think of volunteers as being irresponsible, lacking in initiative and in need of close supervision and restricted independent action than paid staff.

I have personally found this assumption totally unfounded when the right volunteer is selected for a meaningful job and encouraged and enabled to do the job the person is capable of doing, which is exactly what I have found to be true for paid staff.

Louis Allen, President of Louis A. Allen Associates, Inc., in the December 1973 *Personnel Journal,* suggested adding a third theory which he calls "Theory M" (for management). One of the excellent points made was, "Managers are as human as those they manage, as needful of understanding and compassion, as capable of giving, trusting, and loving. Real progress in relationships will occur when both superiors and subordinates try to understand the needs and roles of the other and to work together to develop new and better ways of achieving goals".[6]

Peter Drucker has spent considerable time and effort consulting with and studying successful companies in Japan, Germany and the U.S. He concludes that these organizations base their managing on *organizing responsibility* instead of organizing authority. He views this as the key to successful leadership. In order to establish this climate where work is achievement and fulfillment, not drudgery, he states three ingredients are essential:

1. productive (or real) work;
2. feedback information; and
3. continuous learning.

When these are established, workers take responsibility for their own jobs and the spirit of the organization reflects enthusiasm, creativity and productivity. Drucker strongly encourages worker participation in designing all three of the necessary ingredients from the very beginning.[7]

Another author who agrees with this concept is M. Scott Myers. In his book, *Every Employee A Manager,* which he based on his ten years of management development pioneering at Texas Instruments Corp., he states that the good manager is one who provides a climate in which people have a sense of working for themselves. He illustrates this concept by showing how employees should be involved in the planning and controlling of their work and not just in the doing.[8] We will consider how he suggests doing this in the next Chapter.

This again has direct application for volunteer programs. If volunteers are involved in the planning and the evaluation of their jobs and of the total volunteer program, they have a much greater commitment to it. All too frequently they are forced to work in a vacuum, with little or no information about or influence on how their jobs fit into the whole. Their commitment to you is often in direct correlation to your commitment to them. The same is of course true for paid staff.

As we look at the behavior of leaders, we see a continuum that extends all the way from very authoritarian, task-oriented styles to very democratic or relationship-oriented behavior. This is often illustrated as shown on the chart on the next page.[9]

Climate may seem like a very intangible, almost illusive thing and yet it is possible to measure the climate of an organization, especially as it reflects leadership styles. Rensis Likert developed an instrument which enables group members to rate their organization in terms of its management systems. He divided possible responses into four management systems, ranging from a highly structured authoritarian style, to a relationship-oriented style reflecting teamwork, mutual trust and confidence.[10]

I have adapted Likert's instrument to be particularly applicable to human service agencies or organizations using volunteers and have included it as an appendix to this Chapter. I have used this in various workshop training and problem solving situations, both within my own organization and with other agencies, and have found it to be extremely useful.

One of the most meaningful uses I have found for it is in measuring attitudes of both volunteers and paid staff within the same organization. For example, for a workshop I conducted for a large metropolitan agency which had been having staff-volunteer conflict, we had both groups (25 top level managers and 25 volunteer leaders) complete the questionnaire and turn them in anonymously two weeks prior to our session. We then compiled the results and reflected the composite scores for staff in one color and volunteers in another color on a huge chart which we used as the basis for the day's discussion and problem solving.

It was fascinating, and very helpful to the group to be able to visually grasp the significant differences in opinions of volunteers and paid staff on almost every item. The same 50 people who had completed the questionnaire participated in the workshop and the day was productively spent trying to understand what had caused these differences between staff and volunteers, and then setting goals and objectives that could correct the situation.

Within the Boulder Volunteer and Information Center, we have

64

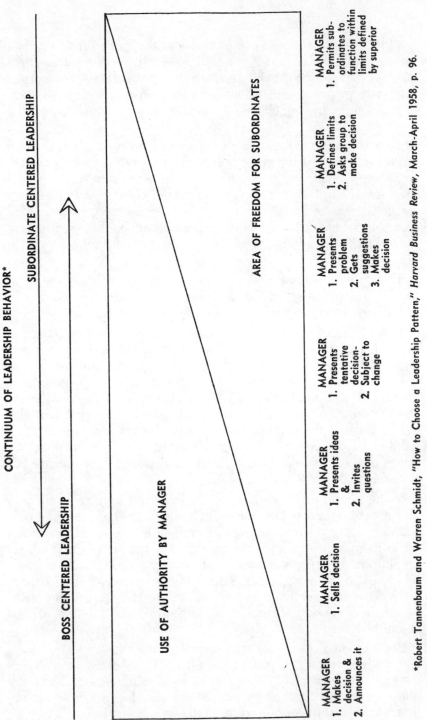

CONTINUUM OF LEADERSHIP BEHAVIOR*

BOSS CENTERED LEADERSHIP

SUBORDINATE CENTERED LEADERSHIP

USE OF AUTHORITY BY MANAGER

AREA OF FREEDOM FOR SUBORDINATES

MANAGER
1. Makes decision & Announces it

MANAGER
1. Sells decision

MANAGER
1. Presents ideas & Invites questions

MANAGER
1. Presents tentative decision-Subject to change

MANAGER
1. Presents problem
2. Gets suggestions
3. Makes decision

MANAGER
1. Defines limits
2. Asks group to make decision

MANAGER
1. Permits sub-ordinates to function within limits defined by superior

*Robert Tannenbaum and Warren Schmidt, "How to Choose a Leadership Pattern," Harvard Business Review, March-April 1958, p. 96.

65

used it both as an evaluative tool and as the basis for future goal setting. I also have used it at training sessions for Volunteer Directors. By completing it twice (once as they presently see their organization or program, and secondly as they wish it were), they can easily identify areas of climate or managerial gaps which need attention.

Two situations which may exist in volunteer programs within large agencies and organizations need to be addressed specifically regarding climate and leadership: 1) the leadership of the agency itself may be autocratic, creating an overall climate of bureaucratic restrictiveness and mistrust, or 2) the climate of a particular department which utilizes volunteers may be unhealthy, creating volunteer/staff difficulties. What can a Director of Volunteers do in either instance?

There are no quick and easy solutions to either problem, but hopefully by recognizing that the situation exists, some strategies can be formulated to at least minimize the negative affects.

In the first instance, the most effective approach may be setting an example in your own Office of Volunteers of the positive results of good climate and leadership (lower turnover, loyal and productive volunteer and staff team members, higher productivity, less absenteeism). It may take time, but almost invariably agency administration and other staff managers are going to notice and wonder why. When you get the opportunity, identify the reasons in a positive, helpful way, suggesting books such as Litwin & Stringer or any others that could help them understand the impact of climate and themselves as managers.

In the second situation, you may find yourself in the role of mediator or arbitrator. As Director of Volunteers, you still have an obligation to those volunteers even after they are referred to another department or program of your agency. The quality of the volunteer program in its entirety is your responsibility. Therefore, you might find initiating joint meetings of staff and volunteers in that department desireable (convincing the manager of the department of the need first, of course). If problems can be aired and solutions arrived at jointly, it is ideal.

But if the manager refuses to deal with the issue, simply be honest and tell him or her that you will be unable to refer any more volunteers to that department for awhile, as good volunteers are being lost to the agency and staff is upset in the process. It is a subtle pressure that is fully within your prerogative to exert, if you will.

Part of the training you do should always be for paid staff on the use of volunteers, and here, too, is an excellent opportunity to introduce the importance of leadership style and climate as they relate to volunteers.

However, actually changing one's managerial style or the climate of an organization is not easy. Understanding how things really are and how they ought to be is important, but making them happen is quite another thing. The only formula I know is commitment and good hard work.

As Scott Meyers said, "The intellectual understanding of management theory has about the same impact on a manager's supervisory style that the intellectual study of snow skiing has on teaching him to ski. In either case, his competence is developed primarily through application".[11] In other words, working at it—not wishing, makes it so.

One final word on leadership and climate. As one studies the vast amount of literature now available in the field of management development, one theme seems to emerge. Effective leadership is contingent upon how well it fits the situation. It is only as the three prime ingredients—people, tasks and leadership are effectively blended together that the climate is going to be conducive to maximum productivity and job satisfaction. This is called the situation or contingency approach to leadership and it makes good, sound sense.

Is climate important? Peter Drucker thinks so, for he states, "it is the spirit of an organization that motivates, that calls upon a man's reserves of dedication and effort, that decides whether he will give his best or do just enough to get by."[12]

References

1. Litwin, George H., & Stringer, Robert A. Jr., *Motivation and Organizational Climate*, Harvard Univ., 1968, p. 5.
2. Ibid, p. 81-82.
3. Ibid, p. 189-90.
4. Hersey, Paul & Blanchard, Kennth H., *Management of Organizational Behavior*, Prentice-Hall, Inc., 1969 & 72, p. 67.
5. McGregor, Douglas, *The Human Side of Enterprise*, McGraw-Hill, 1960.
6. Allen, Louis A., "Beyond Theory Y," *Personnel Journal*, Dec. 1973.
7. Drucker, Peter F., *Management: Tasks, Responsibilities, Practices*, Harper & Row, 1973-74, p. 265-70.

8. Myers, M. Scott, *Every Employee A Manager*, McGraw-Hill, 1970, p. 99.
9. Tannenbaum, Robert & Schmidt, Warren, "How To Choose a Leadership Pattern," *Harvard Business Review*, March-April, 1958, p. 96.
10. Likert, Rensis, *The Human Organization*, McGraw-Hill, 1967.
11. Myers, p. 8.
12. Drucker, Peter F., *The Practice of Management*, Harper & Bros., 1954, p. 144.

PROFILE OF VOLUNTEER-STAFF CHARACTERISTICS*

Instructions:

1. Please mark each item below with an "n" at the point on the scale which in your experience best describes your organization *now*.

2. Then mark each item with a check (X) where you would like to have it be with regard to that item.

Note: Please check if you are: Paid Staff _____   Volunteer _____

I. *LEADERSHIP:*

	System 1 Virtually none	System 2 Some	System 3 Substantial amount	System 4 A great deal
1. How much confidence and trust does staff have in volunteers?	Virtually none	Some	Substantial amount	A great deal
2. How much confidence and trust do volunteers have in staff?	Not very free	Somewhat free	Quite free	Very free
3. How free do you feel to talk to your immediate volunteer or staff supervisor about your job?	Seldom	Sometimes	Often	Very frequently
4. How often are your ideas sought and used constructively by your volunteer or staff supervisor?	Discouraged Almost never occurs	Occasionally occurs	Encouraged most levels	Good at all levels
5. How do you feel about delegation of authority?				

*Adapted by Marlene Wilson from an instrument used in industry (Rensis Likert).

II. MOTIVATION:

	Minimal recognition, personal involvement and achievement	Moderate recognition, involvement and achievement	Frequent recognition, some involvement, marginal achievement	Optimum involvement, personal enrichment and achievement
1. The motivational forces used most in this organization are:				
2. Who feels responsibility for achieving the goals of this organization?	Top administration	Top administration and Board volunteers	Most people who work here	Everyone—admin., staff and volunteers
3. How much cooperative team work exists	Very little	Relatively little	Moderate amount	Great deal
a. between members of paid staff?				
b. between volunteers and paid staff?				
c. between volunteers?				
4. How much satisfaction do you derive from your job and your achievements here?	Very little	Moderate amount	Adequate	Very high

III. *COMMUNICATION:*

1. What is the amount of interaction and communication aimed at achieving the goals?

Very little	Some	Quite a bit	Much, with both individuals & groups

2. What is the usual direction of the flow of information?

Downward	Mostly downward	Down & up	Down, up, and sideways

3. How well do supervisors comprehend problems faced by their volunteers and professional staff?

Not very well	Rather well	Quite well	Very well

4. How would you rate the general communications between staff & volunteers?

Poor	Need more	Adequate	Very good

IV. DECISIONS:

1. At what levels are decisions made?

Mostly at top levels		Policy decisions made at top, some delegation		Broad policy at top, more delegation		Decision making done throughout organization

2. Are volunteers involved in decision making process?

Very seldom		Superficially but not in serious matters		Adequate involvement		Their involvement is sought at all decision making levels

3. Are volunteers and professional staff involved in decisions relating to their work?

	Almost never		Occasionally consulted		Generally consulted		Fully involved
a. Paid Staff							
b. Volunteers							

V. GOALS:

1. How are agency goals established?	By management and staff to volunteers in condescending manner	By Board volunteers to staff in an arbitrary manner	By select management, staff and volunteers in a controlling manner	By management, staff & volunteers in a democratic manner
2. Do you have the opportunity to set goals for your job?	Never	Seldom	Occasionally	Usually
3. How well informed are most members of this organization of the goals?	Know very little	Vague knowledge	Adequately informed	Well informed
4. Are your personal goals being met in your present job?	Not at all	Minimally	Adequately	Very well

VI. GENERAL KNOWLEDGE:

Inhibits initiative and achievement	Sometimes conducive but with many restrictions	Adequately conducive	Extremely conducive

1. *Physical Facilities.* Extent to which the physical facilities and equipment within the office are conducive to creative initiative and achievement.

Inadequate information flow	Information flow adequate	Information flows very well	Keeps everyone well informed

2. Extent to which printed internal communications serve as information tool.

Almost none	Limited	Adequate	Excellent

3. Extent of my personal knowledge and understanding of:

A. the programs of this agency

B. mission and principles of this agency

C. the policies

Negative	Disinterested	Vague	Positive

4. *Image.* Within your personal contacts what response do you get regarding the image of this agency in the community?

CHAPTER V

Planning and Evaluation

A patient in a mental hospital where I once worked spent many busy days knitting a dress. The problem was, although she knew how to knit, she had no plan or pattern for the dress. So day after day she knit, always expecting it to come out looking like the dress she wanted. In reality it was just a very long scarf, getting longer by the day. She refused any advice or help, stating adamantly she knew what she was doing and needed no busybody telling her how to do what she'd done for years. It was not until she decided to try on her dress that she realized it had not turned out as expected at all. And the tragedy was, she could not for the life of her understand why.

The lack of planning is evident in our lives almost every day. Sometimes it is in small, relatively unimportant things (like forgetting the potato chips for a picnic or leaving ski boots home on a ski trip). Sometimes it is in more significant things, like not budgeting for a desk and office supplies for the new office person or arriving at a training session with a new training film without having arranged for a projector and screen.

The point is, if plans have not been thought out ahead of time, frequently inconvenience, ineffectiveness or even disaster can result.

Efforts are misdirected, people disappointed and funds wasted in the process.

In this Chapter we are going to be examining the "Siamese twins" of management—planning and evaluation. Planning is deciding in advance what to do, how to do it, when to do it, and who is to do it. It bridges the gap from where we are to where we want to go, as said in Chapter II. Evaluation is deciding if where we have gone is in fact where we intended to go.

PLANNING

There are a number of terms that are used in most of the literature on planning and it might be helpful if we clarify those at the very beginning:

- —*Goals*—The ends toward which effort is directed; where a person or organization wants to go—its mission or purpose.
- —*Objectives*—The translation of goals and purposes into definite, measurable targets with standards of performance and achievement for both the organization and individuals. (They are sometimes called operational goals.)
- —*Activity*—What needs to be done to achieve objectives.
- —*Plans*—Tactics and sequences of activities to accomplish goals. (Deciding who will do what, when and how.)
- —*Budget*—That part of a plan expressed in numerical and monetary terms.
- —*Schedule*—A plan with timings and staff assignments.
- —*Controls and/or Evaluation*—Measurement of the extent to which actions conform to plans. Determining if plans were implemented successfully.

As you will recall, in Chapter II we outlined the functions of a manager (planning, organizing, staffing, directing and controlling). In the book *Principles of Management*, Koontz and O'Donnell point out that planning is the most basic of these functions, because the other four functions are simply added to help the organization attain the goals and objectives arrived at in planning. For example, they state any attempt to evaluate or control a program without plans would be meaningless since there is no way anyone can tell whether he is going where he wants to go—the task of evaluation—unless first he knows where he wants to go—the task of planning.[1]

But understanding and accepting the concept of planning is far from implementing it, so let's begin to get very practical. What needs to be planned? Who should be involved? When should it be done? How do you plan effectively?

What Needs to be Planned?

The first thing any organization, agency, business or program should do in the planning process is to identify and clearly state its purpose for being or goal. This may be regarded as the reason for this organization's existence, its mission and guiding philosophy. This would form the foundation for all other objectives and plans. It is amazing how many organizations have no such clear statement of purpose or if they do, how many of their paid staff members or volunteers are unable to state it clearly and concisely. And yet it has been found that organizations that do not do this deny their people a significant opportunity to add meaning to their work lives. It is tremendously important that people know how their job fits with and has significance to the overall purpose. It is the difference between working toward a goal and just doing a job.

Ivan Scheier, in his book *Using Volunteers in Court Settings,* emphasizes the importance of this first step when he states, "The guiding philosophy may best be viewed as the general framework within which a given program will operate and the direction such program will ultimately take. At the very least, it is a statement of the basic ideas and goals which govern the planning process."[2]

At the Volunteer and Information Center we formulated such a statement of purpose at the very beginning and it has proven to be invaluable to me, as staff, and to our Board, as policy-makers. It serves as a guide in deciding what projects, procedures and programs we should or should not undertake. Our statement is as follows:

"The Volunteer and Information Center of Boulder County serves the community in two ways. First, the Center acts as a clearing house to recruit, screen and place volunteers in Boulder County in the areas of health, education, recreation and welfare. Secondly, the Center is an information and referral service for persons or groups seeking to locate available resources in the County. Our motto is 'helping others help' by getting need and resources together in every way possible."

All other plans we formulate at VIC must support or enable this general goal and purpose by improving our service or efficiency.

Thus, we have formed a Youth Task Force, Senior Citizens' Task Force, School Aide and Tutor Task Force, 'Do Something' Council (for groups) to help us recruit and place volunteers more effectively, and the Directory Task Force compiles and updates a comprehensive Community Resources Directory which serves as the basis for our information and referral service, and so on.

Once this "reason for being" has been defined, then it is appropriate and necessary to proceed on to setting organizational objectives. Remember objectives are the more specific targets we identify that will help us achieve the overall goals.

It is not uncommon for organizations to confuse broad goals with objectives. To combat this problem, using a system of testing objectives referred to as SMAC, may prove helpful:

S—is it specific?

M—is it measureable?

A—is it achievable?

C—is it compatible with the overall goal and other departmental objectives?

In a Volunteer Directors' workshop in Cincinnati, a manager from Proctor & Gamble presented this concept. He then asked one of the Directors for an objective for his volunteer program. The reply was, "to recruit more teenagers as big brothers for my inner-city program". As the group attempted to apply the SMAC formulae to this, we discovered it was not an objective at all, for it was too general. Restated as a good objective it became "to recruit 25 black junior and senior boys from West High School during the next nine months to work as big brothers in my inner-city program." It was then specific, measurable, achieveable and compatible.

As a part of organizational objectives, it is also important to go beyond *what* do we want to do and include *how* are we going to do it. That includes making a *realistic budget* (how much will it cost), defining appropriate *jobs* and *organizational structure* (who is to do what tasks), and planning *work schedules* (when will it be done). It is a matter of planning your work and then working your plan. We will discuss this later in the Chapter when we deal with "Management by Objectives". One important point to remember here, however, is in defining plans, never overlook the value of examining all alternatives before you decide on which course to pursue. The most obvious is not always the best.

Another part of the planning process relates to the personal goals and objectives of the people who work in the organization. Charles Hughes, who wrote *Goal Setting: Key to Individual and Organizational Effectiveness*, states that there is one purpose that all people in a work situation share, whether it be the president, shop worker, secretary [or volunteer]. That is the purpose of *becoming* or of actualizing the human potential for psychological growth. He says, "Only through one's potential for doing things, using one's abilities, achieving personal goals, can one develop as a human being and learn to be responsible for one's behavior. Man's purpose, in other words, finds expression in achieving individual goals."[3]

This certainly makes clear not only the desirability, but the necessity of goal setting for us as individuals and for each person, paid or volunteer, that works with us. The challenge for the manager then becomes one of helping people to identify and articulate their personal goals and synthesizing these with organizational goals. The two must be compatible if the situation is to be productive and satisfying for both.

M. Scott Myers has identified factors which he feels give meaning to goals and thus inspire people to achieve them. He states,[4]

"Goals which have the maximum motivational value are:

1. Influenced by the goal-setter
2. Visible
3. Desirable
4. Challenging
5. Attainable

and they lead to the satisfaction of needs for

6. Growth
7. Achievement
8. Responsibility
9. Recognition
10. Affiliation
11. Security."

It is important that we help people "stretch" in their personal goal setting and do in our own goal setting as well. Goals must be realistic, surely, but not just sure things or opportunities for growth are lost. Charles Wilson, former President of General Motors, once observed that a good boss makes people realize they have more ability than they think they have, so that they consistently do better work than they thought they could.

And we, as Directors of Volunteers, have a unique opportunity to assist the volunteers who come to us to do meaningful goal setting also. I find the interview with prospective volunteers to be an excellent time to encourage people to explore both long and short range goals, so that we can make their placement as a volunteer in line with those goals . It is astounding how frequently a middle aged woman or retired person will reply, "No one has asked me that for so long. I'll have to go home and think about it and come back later." And they usually do!

It is also crucial to establish goals when young people volunteer, for it is a rare opportunity for them to try out roles and test goal expectations, if placements are made appropriately.

Another kind of individual planning which each of us must be involved in is the every day process of ordering our activities or in other words, deciding what we are going to accomplish today. This becomes a constant process of priority setting and decision making, because there is almost always more to be done than is possible to do in 8 hours.

Charles M. Schwab, one of the first presidents of Bethlehem Steel, asked an efficiency expert to suggest a way to improve the efficiency of his business. The efficiency expert, Ivy Lee, handed Schwab a blank sheet of paper and said, "Write down the six most important tasks you have to do tomorrow. Now number them in the order of their importance.

"The first thing in the morning start working on Number One until it is finished. Then tackle Number Two and so on. Don't be concerned if you have finished only one or two by quitting time. You'll be working on the most important ones. The others can wait. If you couldn't finish them all by this method, you couldn't have done so by any other method, and without some system, you'd probably have failed to finish the most important.

"Do this every working day and after you've convinced yourself of the value of this system, have your men try it. Try it as long as you wish, then send me a check for what you think it has been worth to you."

It is said that a few weeks later Schwab sent Lee a check for $25,000 with a letter saying this lesson was the most profitable he had ever learned.

It is so important to be able to translate goals into action, and to do this we must plan. Goals without plans are dreams.

I have personally found making a simple weekly "TO DO" list is extremely helpful. This seems to have several benefits:

1. Getting it on paper gets it off my mind;
2. It seems more apt to get done and not forgotten;
3. It helps me prioritize my activities; and
4. It directs the attention from what still needs doing to what has already been accomplished. Psychologically it keeps me from feeling harried and developes a sense of accomplishment.

Robert Townsend, the Avis Rent-A-Car wizard, used to keep a sign by his desk that he would look at every time he was about to make an appointment or attend a meeting. It said, "Is what I'm doing or about to do getting us closer to our objective?" He claims that saved him countless trips, lunches, meetings and conferences by keeping him from doing little bits of everything.

Who Should Be Involved in Planning?

There are different opinions about this, depending again on a person's basic assumption about people. Charles Hughes suggests that Theory X managers think goals have been set when each person in the organization knows what is expected of them (top-down goal setting), whereas Theory Y managers think they've been set when each person knows what they expect of themselves, bottom-up goal setting). He concludes, good goal setting is probably a blend of both.

The statement of the purpose of the organization most certainly needs to be determined by the Board of Directors and top management. Then the organizational and individual goals and objectives that help achieve those overall goals can perhaps best be arrived at with meaningful participation by people at all levels. At least this is certainly the premise of the book, *Every Employee A Manager*. In it M. Scott Myers points out that in authority-oriented groups, most workers only get to be involved in the doing of their jobs, not in the planning and controlling of them. He stresses this has a negative effect on motivation, incentive and feelings of achievement. "A job is a job is a job" becomes the attitude.

81

He strongly advocates involving employees (and I would add volunteers) in the total plan-do-control process. An adaptation of his illustration might be:[5]

Authority-Oriented	Goal-Oriented
Set goals for subordinates, define standards and results expected.	Participate with people in problem solving and goal setting.
Give them information necessary to do their job.	Give them access to information which they want.
Train them how to do the job.	Create situations for optimum learning.
Explain rules and apply discipline to ensure conformity; suppress conflict.	Explain rules and consequences of violations; mediate conflict.
Stimulate subordinates through persuasive leadership.	Allow people to set challenging goals.
	Teach methods improvement techniques to job incumbents.
Develop and install new methods.	Enable them to pursue and move into growth opportunities.
Develop and free them for promotion.	
Reward achievements and punish failures.	Recognize achievements and help them learn from failure.

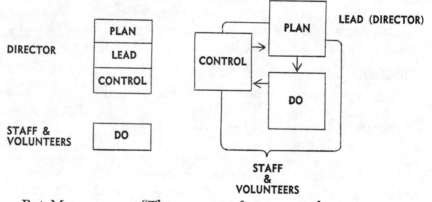

But Myers warns, "The concept of every employee a manager through meaningful work requires supervisory sophistication not common in today's organizations".

In essence then, if we dare to be on the forefront, the answer to our question is—*everybody plans*: administration, staff and volunteers. And they should also include the client in the process. Anyone affected by a plan should have input into it.

When Should Planning Occur?

Hopefully planning occurs before, not after, the fact. It is always disturbing to see people and organizations start out to do a job before they are sure what they want to accomplish. It's like knitting a non-dress.

It has been disconcerting to me how frequently this seems to occur among human service efforts. Countless times I have observed good community people become aware of a particular need (low-cost housing, drugs, environmental abuse, lonely and isolated elderly, etc.) and then immediately pull together a group of other volunteers who set out to "do something about it". The problem so frequently is they do not clearly define the "do something" into actual goals or objectives, and thus run into immediate problems in obtaining funding and community support for their project. This frequently results in still another good idea that failed because of lack of planning. And good potential volunteers are lost in the process.

The simple fact of planning is this—it must be an on-going, constant process because needs change, workers change, communities change, and we must be aware of and responsive to those changes.

It is important to harmonize short term and long range goals and objectives to be sure they are compatible. Something that is expedient today may prove disastrous a year from now. It is helpful to have 1 month—6 month—12 month objectives and then, if possible, integrate these into a long range forecast or plan (i.e., 3-5 years) knowing of course that flexibility is a must to adjust to unforeseen changes. Someone once said "The race goes to the guy who knows where the finish line is and heads for it".

To illustrate how volunteers can be incorporated into this kind of planning, may I use the example once again of a recent situation at our Volunteer and Information Center. A personal goal of mine has been for quite sometime to write this book. I finally realized, when translating this into specific, achievable objectives, that I could not do it while working full time at the Center. I estimated that if I could work two days a week at VIC and write three, I could achieve my goal in six months. I presented this plan to VIC's Advisory Committe(made up of all of our 11 volunteer task force leaders, plus several agency advisors).

They debated the pros and cons of this plan as it might affect the Center and then voted to accept my goal as something they, too, wanted achieved. We then proceeded to meet with each Task Force individually to set specific objectives for each for the next six months. These were all typed and compiled into a document given to each

Advisory Committee member, my supervisor and the Executive Director of United Way (our parent organization). This became our operating manual. The Task Forces have found this most helpful and as a result they have achieved or surpassed all of the objectives set. This also served as an excellent guide for me as Director during my two days at the Center, as it kept me informed of how my time needed to be spent. In fact, it has proven so valuable to all of us, that we intend to continue the practice.

How Is Effective Planning Done?

A frequently used method of planning is called Management by Objectives (MBO). This can be as simple or complex as you wish to make it, but generally it can make planning more effective. In it's simplest form, it is determining WHO is going to do WHAT, HOW and WHEN.

One author defines Management By Objectives as "a process whereby the superior and the subordinate managers of an enterprise jointly identify its common goals, define each individual's major areas of responsibility in terms of the results expected of him, and use these measures as guides for operating the unit and assessing the contribution of each of its members."[7]

Another author states that MBO is "a concept that may be stated in this way; if a manager cannot or does not state, in advance of the time required for action, his objectives in writing and in detail he cannot know for sure what he is doing. As a consequence there can be little hope that his operation will achieve the necessary results so that the fundamental objectives of the organization will be accomplished. *He will not be managing the situation but rather the situation will be managing him.*"[6]

There are four steps:

A. *Prepare*
   1. State objectives clearly and specifically;
   2. Collect facts, opinions and experience of others which may bear on the situation;
   3. Consult with everyone who may be involved directly or indirectly.

B. *Decide*
   1. Analyze all the data, including possible consequences;
   2. Develop alternative courses of action;

    3. Evaluate alternatives and choose the best one;

    4. Set standards.

C. *Communicate*

    1. Determine all who will be affected by the plan;

    2. Select and implement the best method of communicating the plan to them;

    3. Check to be sure everyone understands and accepts the plan.

D. *Control*

    1. Set check points to evaluate the progress on the plan;

    2. Compare actual with anticipated results;

    3. Take remedial action when necessary (change the current plan or even change plans).

Let's create a typical volunteer program situation and "walk it through" this procedure. A juvenile court is considering adding a volunteer probation officer program. It is the idea of one judge and a probation officer. The Director of Volunteers has been directed to set-up such a program.

A. *Prepare*

    1. The Director of Volunteers has a meeting with the judge and probation officer, and together they draft a clear statement of objectives for this new program.

    2. The Director calls the National Center for Voluntary Action's Clearinghouse and asks for information on all such programs presently listed at the Center. The National Information Center on Volunteerism is also contacted. Any courts which presently have such programs in the area are contacted and if possible, visited.

    3. Interviews are held with other judges and probation officers. Some juvenile probationers and their families, and several court volunteers in other programs are consulted. All are asked for opinions and ideas.

B. *Decide*

    1. A committee is formed with at least one member from each affected group (staff, probationer, family, volunteer and judge).

2. This committee reviews the data and opinions gathered in step one and considers the feasibility as well as possible consequences of the new program and weighs pros and cons.

3. All possible alternatives are developed:

    1) Start program as pilot project involving only the one judge and probation officer; or
    2) Implement it in phases; or
    3) Involve the entire juvenile probation department; or
    4) Arbitrarily, make the use of volunteers mandatory in all departments; or
    5) Recommend the program is not feasible at this time, etc.

4. Committee considers all possible alternatives and selects best one. (They decide on implementing the program in phases). Specific objectives and standards are set.

C. *Communicate*

1. Committee is utilized to determine the best method of communicating the new plan to everyone affected: newsletter, group meetings, personal interviews, newspaper and radio, memos to staff.

2. The suggestions are implemented making sure everyone affected is informed appropriately. (i.e., memo and staff meeting for staff; personal intreviews and/or group meetings for probationers and families; radio, TV and newspaper for general public, and group meetings for volunteers).

D. *Control*

1. Part of the original plan decided on in section B should include evaluation. The committee decides to continue to meet monthly and get verbal reports from the Director as they relate to the original objectives.

2. Written questionnaires are developed by the committee to send to random samplings of staff, clients and volunteers every six months.

3. If problems develop, the Director initiates a special meeting to determine if the plan needs to be altered (add more departments to program, recruit more volunteers, do more careful training).

4. The entire program is evaluated at the end of one year and recommendations made to expand, drop, change or leave it as it is.

See Appendices at the end of this Chapter for a suggested planning work sheet, criteria for evaluating your planning and Management by Objectives outline.

Management by Objectives or any other similar planning procedure will keep us from being like Alice in Wonderland. Remember when she said "I don't care where I go" and the cat replied, "Then any road will take you there".

There is another issue closely related to planning that we should examine for a moment. This is how it affects management or leadership style. Many of the books on management talk about "span of control" which is a concept that states that any one person can supervise only a small number of people. It was based on this theory that the typical hierarchical organization chart and bureaucracy was formed. (Layer upon layer of small numbers of people who are responsible to other people, who in turn are responsible to other people, etc.)

Peter Drucker states that *if responsibilities are organized effectively* this theory is not necessarily true. When a person "is controlled by the objective requirements of his own job and measured by his results, there is no need for the kind of supervision that consists of telling a subordinate what to do and then making sure that he does it. There is no span of control." He goes on to say, the only limit is the number of people a manager can *assist, teach* and *help*—and that number varies with the manager and situation.[7]

This has real implications for use of volunteers. If their job and responsibilities are planned well (with them involved in the process), then they too can and should be controlled by the objectives and requirements of the job and evaluated on the results, instead of requiring the constant mothering and close supervision that many Directors of Volunteers and other staff seem to feel is necessary. This would mean not only less staff time required to supervise (which is a staff argument against using volunteers), it would also vastly improve volunteer efforts, outputs and morale.

EVALUATION

Evaluation is the yardstick or thermometer we apply to a program. It determines if what is done is what was intended. It has many names: feedback, assessment, controls. It is as essential to the health of any program (including one involving volunteers) as is planning.

Ivan Scheier states volunteer programs need to conduct the best evaluations possible for three reasons:[8]

1) Increasingly, program sponsors and funders require it, whether they be local, state or national—private or governmental. "We've passed our honeymoon period in which sponsors were willing to wait and hope with us. Now they want the practical justification of known results";

2) Evaluation is the only way we're going to preserve what is good in our programs and improve what is not; and

3) It is important for staff/volunteer morale. Someone cares enough to look carefully at what they are doing.

What Should Be Evaluated?

Koontz and O'Donnell identify three basic steps that are necessary in any process of control or evaluation:[9]

1) Establish standards;

2) Measure performance against those standards; and

3) Correct deviations from standards and plans.

In other words, the better job we have done in planning, the easier the job of evaluation will be. If our objectives and standards are clearly stated (and are SMAC objectives), the process of evaluation becomes a relatively simple determination. Did we achieve those objectives (i.e., recruit and place the 25 black teenage big brothers in nine months) and if we did how well is it working? Also—if we did not, why not and what do we need to do about it? (Did we forget to assign a recruiter to West High or allow enough staff time to achieve the objective?)

As managers and others develop verifiable objectives, stated in either quantitative or qualitative terms, these objectives become the standards against which performance can be measured.

In broad terms, there should be two basic targets of evaluation in a volunteer program: 1) the program itself, and 2) individuals working within the program (both paid and volunteer).

The volunteer program needs to be assessed as to its effectiveness in reaching the goals set for it. Are volunteers enriching and extend-

88

ing paid staff efforts in achieving the purpose of your agency or are they window dressing? Is the money expended on the volunteer program reasonable and justifiable when cost per volunteer is computed? Is the program accepted and supported by staff and administration? Do clients of the agency regard the program as being of value to them?

Some questions suggested in a booklet published by Robert McCreech and the Volunteer Bureau of Boston entitled "Let's Measure Up: A Set of Criteria for Evaluating a Volunteer Program," relate to this issue. They are:

—Does the volunteer program in your agency have the complete support and approval of the administration?

—Does the entire staff understand why volunteers are being used in the agency?

—Are all staff members familiar with the ways in which volunteers are being used and in what areas they will be working?

—Is staff prepared as to what to expect of volunteers?

—Are staff responsibilities in regard to the volunteer program clearly defined?

—Is the staff time necessary for maintaining a volunteer program taken into consideration?

The amount of time given by volunteers, both individually and as a group, is a valuable and necessary assessment component. Simple record sheets (check-in and check-out time sheets) or monthly phone checks with volunteers can provide these figures. Another critical factor is the length of service and turnover rate. When volunteers consistently leave before the completion of their assignments or commitments, or when the average length of service remains only a few months, something needs changing.

In evaluating the performance of individual volunteers and employees, I strongly recommend using the method of setting goals and then evaluating the person on the basis of performance as they relate to those stated goals, as opposed to the usual employee checklist type of evaluation. This should be done every 6-12 months.

Robert Townsend states that everybody must be judged on his performance, not on his looks, or his manners, or his personality, or who he knows or is related to.

Who Do You Ask, Who Asks Them, and When?

Just as planning should involve all persons affected by the plan, evaluation should include all those impacted by the volunteer program: the Director of Volunteers, the volunteers, staff, administration and clients. All should have the opportunity to evaluate the program from their perspective. One tool would be the "Profile of Volunteer-Staff Characteristics" presented in Chapter IV. Other possible questionnaires are presented later in this Chapter.

The person or persons conducting an evaluation varies depending on the size and nature of the program. The Director of Volunteers should take the responsibility for seeing that it is done. The Director does, in fact, conduct an on-going informal assessment constantly. Feedback from staff and volunteers, observation, comments at meetings, volunteer reports, statistics and records all provide a picture of the program as it is.

Periodic formal assessments are very necessary. This is frequently most useful as budgets and goals are being prepared for the following year. This is when it is very appropriate to use questionnaires and/or interviews with representatives from each of the groups mentioned that are affected by the program. Some sample questionnaires are included as an Appendix to this Chapter.

Dr. Ivan Scheier's National Information Center on Volunteerism has developed perhaps one of the most thorough evaluation systems available in our field at the present time. It is called "Basic Feedback Systems for Volunteer Programs" and includes a Scorecard for the total volunteer program and forms for line-staff utilizing volunteers, volunteers, top-management, and clients.

Dr. Scheier states this system provides at least some feedback on how the program is doing and does it at a practical cost in time and money. It also provides the opportunity to compare your program with national norms, which is very useful. To obtain more information, write to NICOV, Box 4179, Boulder, Colorado 80302.

Occasionally it may prove very useful to call in an outside consultant to take an objective and thorough look at the program. This is especially useful when the program is having difficulty. For example when the Board, staff and volunteers are in disagreement, or when administration is seriously questioning the value of continuing the program. It is important to find an evaluator who is knowledgeable about volunteerism and who is not otherwise involved with your organization, so the results can be as unbiased and meaningful as possible. If you pursue this alternative, give the consultant your full support and then *implement the recommendations.*

It is important to evaluate from the beginning, with a planned and varied assessment plan, rather than having an elaborate evaluation once a year. And it should be done when the program succeeds, as well as when it is in trouble. It is important to know why something worked well too. Evaluation enables a group to constantly improve performance. As someone once said, the enemy of the best is not the worst, but the good enough. Our volunteer programs must avoid the dangers of safe mediocrity.

On-going evaluation also enables us to discover and correct problems before they become unmanageable. This of course assumes that we intend to act on the data and insights gained from the whole process. It is a truism that success comes from refusal to accept failure. If there are problems, they can and must be solved.

What Should Be Done With Evaluation Results?

Ivan Scheier summed it up well when he said

—Disseminate
—Discuss
—Do Something
—Don't file

This simply illustrates that results must be acted upon.

It is important to involve representatives of all the groups involved in an evaluation in the discussions of the results and consequent re-planning process (consumer/client, volunteers, staff, administration and Office of Volunteers). Results should be objectively examined, alternative courses of action explored and recommendations made for improvement. Then a plan should be drawn up and, of course, action taken. Be sure that in the course of discussions and planning the strengths of the program are recognized and reinforced as well.

A few final thoughts on evaluation or controls from Peter Drucker might prove helpful.[10]

1. *They must be economical.* Ask yourself what is the smallest number of reports and statistics that are needed to understand and have a reasonably reliable picture of this program.
2. *They must be meaningful.* Measure significant things—never trivia.

3. *They must be appropriate.* When measuring a volunteer program utilize criteria appropriate to volunteers and not salesmen, social workers or agency directors.

4. *They must be timely.* Some events need to have rapid reporting back and others should be assessed after a given time (i.e., 6-12 months.). The important thing is, to recognize which is appropriate for what.

5. *They must be simple.* Complicated evaluations don't work. Instead they confuse people. The method and purpose need to be so clear and simply stated they enable, not prevent people from participating.

6. *They must be operational.* Action rather than information is the goal. Never conduct them to compile data that someone just might find interesting, but does not need to know to do the job better.

Finally, evaluation is that which not only enables but forces us to examine the quality and value of our programs. We must be concerned, not only with how to do the things we do more effectively, but must ask hard questions about why we do them, and what happens as a result.

It is through planning and evaluation that future courses are determined—the dreaming done about what ought to happen. And here is where leadership comes in. Robert Greenleaf states, "A mark of a leader, an attribute that puts him in a position to show the way for others, is that he is better than most at pointing the direction." The ultimate goal of the leader is usually something presently out of reach, something to strive for, move toward or become. But it is so stated by the leader that it "excites the imagination and challenges people to work for something they do not yet know how to do, something they can be proud of as they move toward it."[11]

References

1. Koontz, Harold and O'Donnell, Cyril, *Principles of Management*, McGraw-Hill Book Co., 1955-68, p. 83.

2. Scheier, Ivan H., *Using Volunteers In Court Settings*, U.S. Dept. of of Health, Education and Welfare, J. D. Publication No. 477, p. 7.

3. Hughes, Charles L., *Goal Setting: Key to Individual and Organizational Effectiveness*, American Management Assoc., 1965, p. 20.

4. Myers, M. Scott, *Every Employee A Manager*, McGraw Hill Book Co. 1970, p. 42.

5. Ibid, p. 99.

6. *Manageemnt By Objectives Workbook,* published as a report of seminar held at Cal Tech., 1966.

7. Drucker, Peter F., *The Practice of Management,* Harper & Bros., 1954, p. 139.

8. Scheier, Ivan M., "Everyone Should Evaluate Their Court Volunteer Programs and Everyone Can", National Information Center on Volunteers, Aug. 1971.

9. Koontz & O'Donnell, p. 64.

10. Drucker, Peter F., *Management: Tasks, Responsibilities, Practices,* Harper & Row, 1973-74, pp. 498-500.

11. Greenleaf, Robert, *The Servant As Leader,* Center for Applied Studies, 17 Dunster St., Cambridge Mass., 1972, p. 9.

MANAGEMENT BY OBJECTIVES AND RESULTS

I   **Manager and His
Work Group**

Statement of Role and Mission (R&M's)
The job—Its overall scope in terms of Accountability and Contribution (Is and Ought To Be), (What are We and What Ought to Be), (Nature and Scope of the Job)

II   **Objectives &
Results**

Specified Objectives & Results (O&R's)
—"What is to be Accomplished" —"When is it to be Accomplished" —"Cost/Benefit"—$'s, Man-Hours, Resources

III   **Plan of Action**

Plan of Action—To Achieve Projected Results
—"How" to do it—Program Steps —"Who" to do it—Assignments —"Authority" to do it—Delegation —"When" to start and complete-Schedule

IV   **Review & Improve**

Progress Review & Improvement
—Review Results—Compare Achieved to Projected Results —Analyze Varience—Nature, Extent, Cause —Work Improvements—Opportunities and Priorities —Personal Development—Needs, Opportunities, Career Plans and Programs

APPENDIX B

INFLUENCE—ACHIEVEMENT WORKSHEET*

Following are questions which should be answered when planning how to achieve a goal which requires influencing others:

1. What outcome would you like to see occur?

2. Who must be influenced to have the desired outcome occur?

3. What is your source of influence (power) with the person(s) identified above? (consider the following kinds of power: reward, punishment, expert, identity, legitimate)

4. What will the person(s) do if you have been successful in your attempt to influence?

5. What is your strategy for influencing the person(s) to work toward the desired outcome?

6. What action must occur to achieve the desired outcome? By whom?

7. What is the "pay off" if the desired outcome occurs?
   to you?
   to the person(s) you're attempting to influence?
   to others?

8. What happens if the desired outcome fails to occur?
   to you?
   to the person(s) you're attempting to influence?
   to others?

9. What obstacles, real and potential, must be overcome?
   (consider obstacles in influencing others along with obstacles to achieving the desired outcome)

10. What can be done to avert or minimize the obstacles?

11. How intensely do you want the desired outcome to occurr?

*Form developed by Harvey Wilson, June, 1975.

GOALS—SETTING THEM AND MEETING THEM

(Adapted from Center for Management and Technical Programs—University of Colorado)

Goals	Specific Date	Action Steps	Risk	How to Measure Results	Review Date	Anticipated Obstacles	Steps to Avert or Min. Effects of Obstacles	How Confident Are You of Success

SUGGESTED CRITERIA FOR EVALUATING YOUR PLANNING   23

Criteria	Ratings Inadequate	So-So	Excellent
1. Is your plan based on clearly defined objectives that are in accordance with organizational goals?	□ □ □ □ □ 1 2 3 4 5		
2. Is your plan as clear and simple as the task will permit?	□ □ □ □ □ 1 2 3 4 5		
3. Does your plan provide for the involvement of all appropriate personnel?	□ □ □ □ □ 1 2 3 4 5		
4. Is your planning based on realistic analysis of the forces in the situation?	□ □ □ □ □ 1 2 3 4 5		
5. Has your plan forecast expected conditions?	□ □ □ □ □ 1 2 3 4 5		
6. Does your plan have stability which provides for flexibility?	□ □ □ □ □ 1 2 3 4 5		
7. Is your planning economical in use of human and financial resources needed to implement it?	□ □ □ □ □ 1 2 3 4 5		
8. Can your plan be divided and delegated for efficient implementation?	□ □ □ □ □ 1 2 3 4 5		
9. Are the methods to be used in your plan reliable and up to appropriate program standards?	□ □ □ □ □ 1 2 3 4 5		
10. Does your plan provide for adequate training and development of personnel to accomplish the plan?	□ □ □ □ □ 1 2 3 4 5		
11. Does your plan provide for an appropriate implementation process?	□ □ □ □ □ 1 2 3 4 5		
12. Does your plan provide for continuous review and re-evaluation?	□ □ □ □ □ 1 2 3 4 5		

"The above chart is from the Monograph "Planning for Achieving Goals" by Lowell Hattery and is part of a Management series from the Management Library. Publisher and Copyrighter is Leadership Resources, Inc. and special written permission has been given to reproduce the chart. LRI is located at 6400 Arlington Blvd., Suite 344, Falls Church, Va. 22042."

APPENDIX E

EVALUATION OF ADMINISTRATOR BY STAFF/VOLUNTEERS

1. Do you feel you receive adequate support from the Director?

2. Do you feel you have ample opportunity to have input into the operation of the program?

3. Do you feel decisions regarding yourself and your assignment has been discussed properly and implemented with your approval?

4. Are you satisfied with conditions under which you fulfill your assignments or should there be improvement?

5. Do you feel you have satisfactory opportunities to discuss any problems which occur with the administration?

6. Are there any ways that cooperation between administration-staff-volunteers could be improved?

7. Do you feel decisions are made from a fair and informational view-point as opposed to whim or impulse?

8. Do you feel that the administration utilized time to the best advantage?

9. Are there any areas relative to the administration of the program here-to-fore not covered, about which you would care to comment?

*Developed by Evalyn Lyons of RSVP program in Wichita, Kansas.

APPENDIX F

QUESTIONNAIRE FOR VOLUNTEERS

The Boulder Volunteer and Information Center would appreciate your taking the time to complete this questionnaire. The information will be used in choosing program priorities for an Agency/Volunteer Workshop planned for October to which you will be invited. All replies will be held in strictest confidence.

(1) What agencies are you associated with?

(2) Why are you a volunteer?

(3) Are your own needs being met?

(4) How effectively do you feel your skills are now being utilized?

(5) What have been your happiest experiences as a volunteer?

(6) What was disappointing and what could be done about it?

(7) How do you feel about the job you are now doing?

(8) What would you like to learn in order to do a better job?

(9) What would you like to see included in the volunteer/agency workshop?

APPENDIX G

A SUGGESTED EVALUATION TOOL FOR COURT VOLUNTEER PROGRAMS

(Developed by Ivan Scheier, National Information Center on Volunteers, Inc.)

A. STAFF REACTIONS TO VOLUNTEER PROGRAM

This questionnaire is not just to make more paperwork for you. It's because we want your frank ideas on the improvement of our volunteer program .

1. How long have you had any sort of contact with the volunteer program?
2. How much time during an average week are you in any sort of contact with volunteers?
3. How do you see your main role in relation to volunteers? (direct supervisor; they work with cases I also work with; they help with routine around the office, etc.) Please specify.
4. Could the agency use more volunteers now? Fewer volunteers? About the same number?
5. How could volunteers do their present jobs better?
6. What jobs, if any, could volunteers usefully perform that they don't now?
7. Could any jobs volunteers now perform probably be done better or more efficiently using paid staff?
8. What are some of the things you see as particularly helpful in the volunteer program?
9. What are some of the things that could be improved?
10. Any other comments you'd care to make would be most welcome.

B. VOLUNTEER REACTIONS TO VOLUNTEER PROGRAM

We need your help again—your ideas to help us improve our volunteer program.

1. How long have you been in the volunteer program?
2. Please describe briefly your volunteer job(s).
3. Where does your volunteer time go in an average month?
   _____ hours with offender, or otherwise on the job
   _____ hours consulting with regular staff
   _____ hours in various volunteer meetings
   _____ hours filling out reports, paperwork (not part of job itself)
4. What are the main reasons you joined up as a volunteer?
5. What are some of the main satisfactions you're getting from your volunteer work now?
6. What are some of the main frustrations?
7. What do you see as some of the good things about the whole volunteer program now?
8. What do you see as some of the things that could be improved?
9. Please describe any suggestions you may have on useful new jobs volunteers might fill in this program.
10. Any other comments you'd care to make would be most welcome.

C. PROBATIONER REACTIONS

We'd appreciate your help. We hope you'll give us your ideas on how the volunteer program can be made better for all of us. Thanks a lot.

1. What are some of the good things volunteers do that help you?
2. What are some of the things volunteers do that maybe don't help quite as much?
3. What are some new things volunteers could do that would be good?
4. Are there any ways you could help volunteers in their work? What are some of these things, please?
5. Anything else you'd like to say about the volunteer program, please just write it here.

99

CHAPTER VI

Designing Jobs and Recruiting To Fill Them

In this Chapter we deal with two essential components of any type of volunteer program—job design and recruitment. In other words, what do we want volunteers to do and how do we find them?

The use of the word "designing" in the title is intentional. It is not just a more sophisticated way of saying writing job descriptions, for by definition design means "to plan and fashion artistically and skillfully." The jobs we ask volunteers to do within our organizations should merit this kind of attention and creativity, but how frequently do they get it?

Harriet Naylor states "to volunteers we owe an opportunity for self-development, enjoyment, and actualization of ideals and aspirations. To the organizations we are responsible for continuity and vitality of the program and progress toward stated goals . . . both as a means of accomplishing the purposes and ideals of the organization".[1]

It is important to consider job design before recruitment, for you must know *why* you need volunteers before you try to enlist their

101

help. Frequently, however, organizations (especially new ones), concentrate their first efforts on recruitment, in a sort of frenzy to obtain man-power. They come to our Volunteer & Information Center, which serves as a volunteer bureau, and state that they need ten, fifteen, —or even fifty volunteers. When we begin to explore this with them in order to determine what these volunteers are to do, there is often a hesitant, general statement such as, "Well we need them to help us get our program off the ground." We then explain we cannot recruit volunteers for them until they provide us with written job descriptions so that we might refer appropriate volunteers.

Recruiting before designing jobs is rather like trying to dance before the music begins. The possibility of ending up out of step is very good indeed.

JOB DESIGN

Perhaps the first thing to recognize about job design is that it needs to be interwoven carefully into the total fabric of the organization. The other essential threads are *planning* (What do clients need? What will staff accept? Why do you need volunteers?); *leadership style* (What will you delegate and how will you supervise?); and, *organizational climate* (Will volunteers want to work there?). These things will have a significant effect on the number and kinds of jobs you should design, for the jobs must be congruent with the whole.

If, for example, you or the person supervising the volunteer operate out of Theory X assumptions about people (they are lazy, irresponsible and need close direction), and therefore manage in a relatively autocratic style, do not design heavily responsible, achievement oriented jobs . Of, if you hold Theory Y assumptions, do not design your jobs to require close and constant supervision, for your management style will likely not provide it.

Litwin and Stringer provide some helpful guidelines for determining the motivational demands of tasks which will be helpful both in designing jobs and in making suitable placements to fill them.[2] (These relate to the McClelland material presented in Chapter III.)

TASK ANALYSIS

Is it an Achievement Task?

1. How much latitude does a worker have in setting his work pace and work methods?

2. How much choice does a worker have when it comes to getting help or direction from someone else?
3. To what degree does errorless and efficient performance contribute to increased sales or company profits [or agency effectiveness]?
4. To what extent does the task challenge the abilities and skills of the worker?
5. Does the task provide clear, unambiguous feedback about the the quality of performance?

Is it a Power Task?

6. How much opportunity does a worker have to personally direct his co-workers?
7. How much time is available for personal interaction while working?
8. To what degree does the task require the worker to deal directly with his superior?
9. How much control does the worker have over his work pace and work methods?
10. How many times can the worker leave his work area without reprimand?

Is it an Affiliation Task?

11. How many people *must* the worker interact with every two hours?
12. How many people *can* the worker interact with in his working area?
13. How dependent is successful task accomplishment on the cooperation of co-workers?
14. How much time is available for personal nontask interactions while working?
15. To what extent does the task allow for maintenance of stable working relationships?

It is when we are able to match the motivational needs of people who work with us to appropriate jobs that need to be done that we see both motivation and performance improve perceptively. To discern the needs of people, simply *ask them* or *observe them.*

Part of the difficulty has traditionally been with the character of work itself. The tendency in industry, as well as many bureaucratic organizations, has been to divide work into the smallest possible segments and then have everyone specialize in performing one or more of these tasks. This is how mass production and assembly lines emerged.

In *Job Design for Motivation,* the authors point out that after World War II research began to try to better understand work and work motivation. Both technical and sociological implications were considered, but most frequently the studies were viewed in terms of "man's adjustment to the system rather than of redesign of the systems to meet man's needs".[3]

This was partially true because the old ways of organizing work in industrial settings had been successful in an economic sense. Business was booming, so why change!

Robert Townsend, in *Up the Organization,* graphically portrays why change is necessary. He states "In the average company the boys in the mailroom, the president, the vice-presidents and the girls in the steno pool have three things in common: they are docile, they are bored, and they are dull. Trapped in pigeonholes of organization charts, they've been made slaves to the rules of private and public hierarchies that run mindlessly on and on because nobody can change them. So we've become a nation of office boys. Monster corporations like General Motors and monster agencies like the Defense Department have grown like cancer until they take up nearly all the living working-space. Like clergymen in Anthony Trollope's day, we're but mortals trained to serve immortal institutions."[4] But he calls on those with courage, humor and energy to make these monster organizations operate as if people were human.

And Mr. Townsend is not the only one to sound a discouraging word regarding work today. In a recent survey, *Work in America,* 50-60% of Americans said they were dissatisfied with the work they are doing. And Studs Terkel in his current best-selling book, *Working,* states that the specter that haunts most working men and women today is this, "the planned obsolescence of people that is of a piece with the planned obsolescence of the things they make. Or sell. It is perhaps this fear of no longer being needed in a world of needless things that most clearly spells out the unnaturalness, the surreality of much that is called work today."[5]

Dr. Saul Gellerman states that if management is to stop the trend toward the dehumanization of work and tap man's potential more fully, it must shape the work environment (including the work itself) into a stimulus, not a suppressor.

Today's more affluent, educated and sophisticated work force is demanding change and are showing this in ways ranging all the way from apathy to rebellion. As the lower levels of need have been satisfied, the need for work to be more than survival becomes very real. People will no longer work long and hard at jobs that offer no challenge or meaning. They say, together with Abraham Maslow, "what's not worth doing isn't worth doing well." According to experts, the changes occuring in both work and worker in the last half of this century are the most radical changes since the beginning of the industrial revolution over 200 years ago. And the volunteer work force is demonstrating these same characteristics of restiveness and discrimination in their choice of volunteer work. Busy work, even for a good cause, is still busy work and entails little motivation or satisfaction.

Drucker states that a job that is too small is an insidious, slow poison which paralyzes both the person and the organization. "A job should be specific enough so that a man can go to work on it, but so big that he can't get his arms around it."[5] This is another way of saying enlarge the opportunity and the person will expand to fill it.

And Townsend points out that in America the first three levels of need on Maselow's hierarchy (physiological, safety and social) are pretty well satisfied in much of today's work force. "But we're still acting as if people were uneducated peasants. Much of the work done today would be more suitable for young children or mental defectives. And look at the rewards we're offering our people today: higher wages, medical benefits, vacations, pensions, profit sharing, bowling and baseball teams. Not one can be enjoyed on the job. You've got to leave work, get sick, or retire first. No wonder people aren't having fun on the job."[6]

And think of our volunteers! They don't even get the rewards that paid staff does, so if they don't get satisfaction in the work they do, they don't get anything at all.

As we grapple with this problem of how to change or arrange the work in our organizations so it will be more humane, interesting (and fun) and at the same time more productive and meaningful, perhaps

105

we need to review what Herzberg stated about motivation (Chapter III). Remember, he identified "motivators" as:

—Achievement
—Recognition
—Challenging work
—Increased responsibility
—Growth and development

When we integrate this into the realm of volunteer programs we can see obvious implications not only for how we design jobs, but for problems we may be having in recruiting for jobs we presently have, or in turnover of current volunteers. Do our volunteer jobs entail any or all of Herzberg's motivators? If not, why not?

Someone once observed that many managers are "people shrinkers" and one of the most effective ways this can be accomplised is to under-utilize people's potential. Do the jobs we offer, both paid and volunteer, offer opportunity for achievement of *meaningful* work, a chance for growth, learning and increased responsibility? How tragic it would be if we in the field of human services do ourselves diminish, rather than build, those who offer their services through us to others.

But, you might ask, what about those routine, sporadic tasks that are necessary and that seem to be all certain volunteers want (i.e., filing, once-a-month mailings, rolling bandages). You are right, there are some volunteers who are perfectly happy to do those jobs and really want no more, due to time limitations, family responsibilities, level of self-confidence, etc. The danger is that we sometimes make assumpitons about the volunteers without checking those assumptions out with them. And this must be done not only at the time of placing the volunteer but periodically, for people and situations change. (The children go to kindergarten, the self-confidence improves, the job becomes dull.) The option to move out of such positions must be a viable one and one which the volunteers realize is open to them. Just knowing we have options is extremely comforting to all of us. This is not to suggest that volunteer jobs are either all routine, repetitive tasks or all high-level, responsible jobs. As in paying jobs, most are a mixture of both. The question is, how much of each is appropriate for each volunteer.

Recognizing that there are different kinds of jobs we need done and different levels of commitment on the part of volunteers suggests to me we must be flexible both in the types of jobs we offer and how we define them. Some volunteers are capable and willing to assume very responsible assignments. These would probably be either volunteer board members or administrative volunteers. I will be dealing with Boards and Advisory Committees in the last Chapter so will deal only with the latter at this time.

I would strongly urge that the design of administrative or "volunteer professional" type of positions should define the *broad areas of responsibility* to be delegated. It is not necessary to spell out the specific tasks required to fulfill these responsibilities, nor necessarily the time and manpower needed. The good volunteer should have the authority and freedom to decide *how to do the job*. How much time will it take, do they need help and if so, do they want to recruit it themselves, or have the Volunteer Director do it? This can be decided in the mutual goal setting sessions with the Director of Volunteers, or the department supervisor, after the volunteer accepts the assignment.

An example would be to assign a volunteer the responsibility of recruitment of volunteers for your program. You would decide, before interviewing for this position, what abilities and skills the person should possess (PR experience, speaking ability, organizational skills, etc.) When you find a volunteer with these capabilities and an interest in and commitment to your agency's goals, hopefully you could interest her in the job. One of the key considerations at this point for the good volunteer is—have you already defined and designed the whole recruitment campaign and really only want a "mechanic" to carry it out. Or, are you really delegating the design and implementation of the recruitment responsibility. In the first instance, you are delegating tasks; in the second, responsibility.

The less responsible the job, the more specific you should be in your job descriptions as to time, duties and details. The volunteers interested in these jobs really need to know exactly what is expected in order to make decisions as to time available and skills needed, to know if it fits with the realities of their lives at that moment.

Perhaps we could illustrate it like this:

MOST RESPONSIBLE VOLUNTEER JOBS

Define broad areas of responsibility and authority.
Assign responsibility, not specific, detailed tasks.
Allow person to negotiate time and manpower needs.
Skills and abilities required should be defined.
Leave room for initiative and creativity in
how responsibility is carried out.

LESS RESPONSIBLE JOBS

Task generally spelled out fairly
well. Time and skills required
are defined. Lines of re-
sponsibility and authority
indicated.

LEAST RESPONSIBLE
JOBS

Duties, time and
skills clearly
defined. Much
more speci-
fic re
tasks-
exactly
what
needs
to be
done
and
when

Example of MOST RESPONSIBLE VOLUNTEER POSITION

TITLE: Volunteer Recruitment Task Force Leader (or Chairman)

RESPONSIBLE TO: Director of Volunteers

AREA OF RESPONSIBILITY: To be responsible for the recruitment of volunteers for this agency. This includes the organization of other volunteers to assist in this outreach effort as needed; the design of recruitment materials; and the implementation of recruitment objectives, as defined together with the Director of Volunteers and approved by the Advisory Committee.

LENGTH OF COMMITMENT: One (1) year

QUALIFICATIONS: Organizational skills, knowledge of public relations and ability to work well with staff and other volunteers. Knowledge of the community helpful.

COMMENTS: This position carries a good deal of responsibility and thus it is recommended that it be your only (or at least, major) volunteer commitment for this year.

Example of LESS RESPONSIBLE VOLUNTEER POSITION

TITLE: Speaker's Bureau Volunteer

RESPONSIBLE TO: Volunteer Recruitment Task Force Leader

DEFINITION OF DUTIES: Give presentations and/or speeches on behalf of this agency for the purpose of recruiting more volunteers and encouraging community support of our organization and its goals. Speeches to be given at service clubs, churches and other interested groups as assigned by Recruitment Task Force Leader.

TIME REQUIRED: 2-4 hours per month. Generally audiences would meet over lunch or dinner hours, but not always.

QUALIFICATIONS: Public speaking; ability to operate visual aide equipment helpful. Commitment to this agency's goals and objectives and a belief in the value of volunteers. Enthusiasm a must.

TRAINING PROVIDED: Orientation sessions will be arranged with staff and volunteers to thoroughly acquaint volunteer with this agency, the volunteer program and the needs of both.

Example of LEAST RESPONSIBLE VOLUNTEER POSITION
TITLE: Telephone Aide

RESPONSIBLE TO: Volunteer Recruitment Task Force Leader and Secretary

DEFINITION OF DUTIES: To telephone prospective volunteers from lists obtained at speeches and presentations to set up interviews with the staff. Phoning should be done at the Office of Volunteers.

TIME REQUIRED: 2 hours a week. Monday a.m. preferred.

QUALIFICATIONS: Pleasant phone personality and ability to work congenially with staff and volunteers.

COMMENTS: This volunteer must have transportation available, as our agency is not accessible by public transportation.

The best job descriptions are not elaborate and complicated, but precise and concise. The epitomy of this was the description for the job of a cymbal player—where the person filled in the question "What does he need to know?" with "Nothing except *when*."

But what do we do about jobs that already exist? Should we leave them alone, as long as someone is filling them, and assume all must be well?

To answer that, perhaps we should look again to researchers who are involved in the job-design-for-motivation movement. There seems to be several common statements they agree upon:[7]

1. Most jobs can be improved;
2. Job content is related to job satisfaction;
3. Motivation is directly related to job satisfaction and personal freedom to work on a self-sufficient independent basis;
4. Job design can be a means for individual and organizational growth;
5. Motivation and productivity are inextricably linked; and,
6. Man seeks and needs meaningful work and the opportunity for creative expression.

Based on the first statement alone, perhaps this would be a good time to objectively and critically examine all our jobs, and most certainly those we find difficult to fill or that are plagued with repeated volunteer turnover.

If we find our present jobs to be lacking in Herzberg's motivators, or if we are finding recruitment to be more and more difficult, there are several methods we can use to improve the design of our jobs: *job enlargement, job enrichment* or *work simplification.*[8]

1. *Job Enlargement.* Sometimes job satisfaction can be increased by simply increasing the number and variety of things a person does. It *widens* the number of tasks for which they're responsible. (However, a word of caution: two or three meaningless activities do not add up to a meaningful one.)

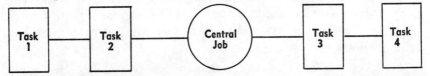

For example, a hospital volunteer who pushes a book cart may also be able to work with the library to get more loaned books or the auxillary in getting additional used ones; take special requests for books from the library for long term patients; and even return to read to patients who are unable to read after the book cart rounds are completed.

2. *Job Enrichment.* This usually refers to delegating to the person some functions that were generally thought to be managerial. As you recall, we referred earlier to M. Scott Myers' model of Plan-Do-Control, and this is simply a means of enriching a job by allowing the worker to participate in the planning and evaluating of the job, as well as the doing. It *deepens* a person's responsibility for his work.

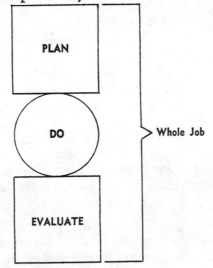

An example here would be involving a public relations volunteer in the planning of what the PR program for the year should be (based on meetings and interviews with staff and volunteers); determining how those PR objectives should be implemented; performing the actual PR functions (or getting other volunteers to assist); and evaluating the results periodically so problems can be averted or corrected and new plans formulated. That volunteer feels a sense of ownership and with it a sense of commitment to that job far greater than if he or she were just instructed to carry out what someone else had planned.

We may tend to assume that this process of job enrichment is only valid for the more responsible jobs. That is not true. Texas Instruments in Dallas designed a major job enrichment program for its janitors and cleaning matrons in 1967. They included all the affected employees in the project and involved them in the Plan-Do-Control aspects of the entire cleaning operation. After $2\frac{1}{4}$ years, they experience the following remarkable results.[9]

1. The cleanliness level rating improved from 65% to 85%;
2. Personnel required for cleaning dropped from 120 to 71;
3. Quarterly turnover dropped from 100% to 9.8%.
4. Cost savings averaged $103,000 per annum.

This illustrates again what Harvey Wilson, the Vice President of Personnel & Administration of Arapahoe Chemicals, a Division of Syntex Corp. observed: "Our attempts to make more meaningful work for all our people are rooted in a basic belief that success depends upon employee involvement in: the design and content of the jobs they perform; fuller participation in decision-making that affects them personally and application of individual creativity in working toward the company's overall objectives. I'm convinced that any employee, whether he is a Ph.D., or a factory worker, has something to contribute to the job to make it more challenging and interesting for himself. The chances are pretty good too, that in doing so he can improve the operation of the larger organization."[10] And it works with volunteers just as well.

3. *Work Simplification.* This is taking a long look at a job to determine if tasks involved can be combined or even eliminated. There could be many useless tasks that still remain, not because

they are needed, but because "we've always done it that way". I can think of several volunteer jobs like that.

This is something that is important for managers as well, for much of our own time is wasted on "administrivia"—paper pushing, report writing, meeting going, etc., that may have had meaning at sometime, but is simply a matter of habit now. What would happen if that memo is not written or that set of statistics compiled? Who will miss them or what will suffer 3-6 months from now if they are not done? Weeding out useless motions is a painful task, yet essential if our programs are to grow and flourish.

It may be we will find whole jobs that can be eliminated—jobs that no longer have any real meaning or value. For example, Dr. Robert Sobel, Associate Professor of History at Hofstra University, says that the British created a civil service job in 1803. This job was for a man to stand on the cliffs of Dover with a spyglass and a bell, which he was to ring if he saw Napoleon coming. The job was abolished in 1945.

If you repeatedly have difficulty in finding volunteers to do a certain job, perhaps the job doesn't deserve to be done in the first place. It is worth considering.

Let us turn for just a moment to the whole process of deciding what jobs need to be done, whether by volunteers or staff. It is important to begin with the overall goal or mission of the organization, then move to setting objectives for how those goals can be accomplished and finally to making specific plans to implement the objectives. These break down into activities and jobs—(who will do what?).

Perhaps we could illustrate it this way:

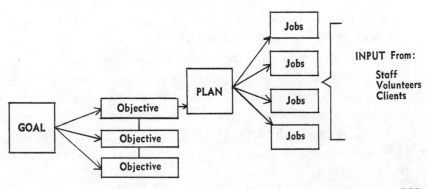

If we follow this sequence, we are more likely to avoid meaningless or unnecessary jobs and to be sure the jobs we do design are appropriate for accomplishing goals and objectives. In this process, we must always keep in mind that good volunteer jobs are 1) *needed by the agency or client,* 2) *wanted by staff, and* 3) *feasible for the volunteers.*

In volunteer programs, the other dilemma is always which jobs are appropriate for paid staff and which for volunteers. There is no magic formula I can suggest, except the basic premise held by most leaders in the field—volunteers should enrich and extend the work of paid staff, never replace it. There is a distinct difference between supplementing and supplanting staff.

Harriet Naylor points out "Highly trained professionals have ranging degrees of interest, skill and experience, as do workers with less competence and education who hold less demanding jobs. The services of highly trained and able professional staff we do have can be extended in geometric proportion if able volunteers can share the supplementary responsibilities which are appropriate to their talents, skills and interests. Some mechanical routines can be carried by paid workers who do not have professional qualifications . . . the existence of voluntarism is important to both volunteers and staff: in our communities for the task to be done, and in our democratic culture for the quality of the doing. It behooves us each to bring out the best in the other."[11]

But for the reluctant or fearful staffs, perhaps some more specific values of accepting the volunteer as a co-worker is in order. In the Goodwill handbook series published in 1973 entitled *Volunteers In Rehabilitation,* some of the benefits of involving volunteers were listed as:[12]

1. *Increased services to clients,* including more time, greater variety of services and more individualized programs;
2. *Providing a bridge between clients and the community;*
3. Providing a vital rehabilitation component—*someone who really cares* (even though they are not paid to do so);
4. *Community understanding and cooperation;*
5. *Social Action—Advocacy* (in legislation at local, state and federal levels);
6. *Fund raising;*

114

7. *Administrative and clerical assistance;*

8. *Technical assistance and professional consultation;* and,

9. *Bringing people together—*clients, staff, volunteers and the community.

And thus comes the plea for cooperation, not competition, between staff and volunteers. Each bring a unique and needed dimension to the delivery of human services. If we can truly understand and accept this, then we can move foreward as a team to meet the ever growing needs of our communities. We will again address this crucial and sensitive issue in the final chapter of this book.

To sum up this section on job design, I again quote Peter Drucker. "Few words in the language are as ambivalent as 'work', and as emotion laden . . . work is complex and embedded in man's life, in his emotions, in his existence in society and community and in his relationship to himself. Working is done by a human being, a worker . . . and is therefore physiology and psychology, society and community, personality, economics, and power. As the old human relations tag has it, 'One cannot hire a hand; the whole man always comes with it'."[13]

RECRUITMENT

I am going to spend a minimum of time and attention on this subject because I truly believe the best recruitment tools are a good, sound volunteer program and meaningful jobs. We have just dealt at length with the latter—and the former is the subject of this entire book, so here we will concentrate on just a few general suggestions:

1. *Do specific, rather than general recruiting whenever possible.* Some generalized PR is necessary to acquaint the community at large with your program and to establish both visibility and credibility. However, few volunteers are recruited this way. It is better to:

   a. *Choose appropriate audiences whose interests and priorities match your needs.* For example, most service clubs have yearly priorities determined by their national organizations. If the priority for Kiwanis is senior citizens this year, an appeal for youth workers may not be appropriate.

   Likewise, it is futile to appeal to a club of business and professional women for day care aides, as they all work when that agency needs the help.

115

b. *Determine where the skills are that you need and actively seek them out.* If you need a brochure done, seek help from an advertising agency or club or from the college art department. If you are starting a program for children with learning disabilities, try ex-teachers, psychology students and parents of the children, (they have the basic skills needed, plus a real interest in learning more about the problem). If you wait for volunteers to find you instead of actively seeking them out, the results are usually disappointing.

c. *Be as specific and honest in your appeal as possible.* What is your need and why? The usual general plea of "we need your help" is getting more and more ineffective, because so many groups and causes need help. As volunteers become more selective and concerned about the value of involvement, they become more insistent upon knowing what skills you need, when and why, so that they can make intelligent decisions as to whether they fit that need or not. And be honest about how much time and what type of work the volunteer job will entail. A glamorous snow-job or the casual "it will hardly take any of your time at all" are danger signals to a good volunteer.

2. *Have a year-round recruitment plan.* Most agencies find early fall and January to be their most fruitful recruitment months for community adults. (Many people determine their yearly schedule of involvement after the children are in school or after the start of a new year.)

Students, both college and high school, are more likely to volunteer during the summer, so a late spring recruitment is often quite productive for them. However, many schools are now giving academic credit for community involvement and if this is possible in your community, the appropriate classes should be contacted in early September and January also. Some universities have Volunteer Bureaus, and if so, they do large, general recruitments in the fall and in January.

During the slower recruitment months, you should still plan speeches, human interest news stories, brochures, etc., because there is often a lag time involved. The prospective volunteers you speak to today may actually be free and ready to volunteer 3, 6 or 12 months from now, so be consistent and year around in your efforts.

3. *Utilize a variety of recruitment techniques.* Certain approaches will appeal to one person, another to others, so try variety and creativity. Some of the possible techniques are:

—*Newspapers*: feature and news stories; ads; volunteer opportunity column; picture coverage of volunteers at work.

—*Radio & TV*: Public service spots (free); interview or talk shows; news stories.

—*Posters, billboards or bumper stickers.*

—*Presentations and Speeches*: to service clubs, church groups, high school and college classes, professional organizations, special interest clubs (use visual aids whenever possible).

—*Brochures and other printed material.*

—*Displays*: utilize slides, pictures, posters and possibly hand out novelty buttons. (This is appropriate at fairs, shopping centers, business or company lobbys.)

—*Person-to-person*: Personal friends of staff or volunteers on a one-to-one basis or at a coffee, brunch or social event. (*Perhaps the most effective approach of all!*)

—*Tours and Open Houses.*

—*Literature or notices* to attract hard-to-reach volunteers in laundromats, grocery stores, bowling alleys, adult education classes, community and youth centers, manpower and employment offices.

—*Newsletters.*

4. *Be sure to utilize the services of the Volunteer Bureau, Voluntary Action Center, or Retired Senior Volunteer Program (RSVP), in your community.* They are there to help you and the volunteer find each other. They can help you best if you submit written job descriptions to them, so they know specifically what you need.

5. *Recruit by inviting people to respond to the opportunity to volunteer, not by telling them they ought to be concerned and involved.* Hopefully, if the jobs you have designed are meaningful, based on all the criteria discussed in this Chapter, you can enthusiastically approach your audience with a real offer of opportunity to serve, to grow and to make a difference.

6. *Be enthusiastic!* If you are not committed to or excited about your program, no one else will be either. And most certainly

lack of enthusiasm will not attract or inspire volunteers to want to help.

7. *Opportunities to volunteer must be expanded to all segments of the community*—it is consistent with the concept of equal opportunity. Instead of being the privilege of the already privileged, volunteering must become the right of everyone: minorities, youth, seniors, the handicapped, blue collar workers, business people, the disadvantaged. Remember—those who understand the culture and life styles of those you are trying to recruit make the best recruiters.

Perhaps our final consideration regarding the recruitment of volunteers might well be to re-think what volunteers identify as being important to them. This should have impact on how we attempt to recruit them. According to the Goodwill handbook entitled *How to Motivate Volunteers* the following are frequently stated reasons for volunteering. Each volunteer brings with them a unique combination or pattern of one or more of these or other motivations that we need to understand and speak to:[14]

—the desire to utilize special knowledge and skills;
—the need for a sense of security that results from feeling one's life has purpose, meaning and significance;
—the need to be a part of activities that have neighborhood, community, regional or national importance;
—the desire to help others;
—the desire for recognition and status;
—the need to feel useful and needed;
—an interest in learning new skills and participating in enjoyable and rewarding activities;
—the desire to gain visibility and skills that will help advancement in employment and social arenas;
—the need to actively utilize leisure time and reduce loneliness, isolation and pressure.

What this recognizes is that the lines between "helper" and "helpee" are almost non-existent, for we now recognize the volunteer and client do indeed help each other—just in different ways.

In conclusion let me say, our efforts to design good volunteer opportunities and to recruit capable and committed people to fill them are tasks worthy of our best efforts. As Harriet Naylor so aptly put

118

it, "the imponderable gift of service is an essential part of the American culture . . . it is the core of idealism which must be preserved if we are not to be dehumanized and voluntarism is not to go altogether. The opportunity to give of one's self is essential to the life of the individuals as well as of the community."[15] Our job is to open up this opportunity of giving to everyone!

References

1. Naylor, Harriet H., *Volunteers Today: Finding, Training and Working With Them*, Dryden Assoc., 1967-73, p. 75.

2. Litwin, George H., and Stringer, Robert A. Jr., *Motivation and Organizational Climate*, Harvard University, 1968, p. 175-76.

3. The Conference Board, *Job Design for Motivation*, Conference Board Report No. 515, p. 5.

4. Townsend, Robert, *Up The Organization*, Fawcett Publications, Inc., 1971, p. XI.

5. Drucker, Peter F., *Management: Tasks, Responsibilities, Practices*, Harper & Row Publishers, 1973-74, p. 411.

6. Townsend, p. 121-22.

7. *Job Design for Motivation*, p. 9.

8. Ibid, p. 12-14 and 43.

9. Ibid, p. 43.

10. Ibid, p. 38.

11. Naylor, Harriet H., p. 15.

12. Levin, Stanley, *Volunteers in Rehabilitation*, Goodwill Industries of America, 1973. .

13. Drucker, Peter F., p. 168.

14. Levin, p. 13.

15. Naylor, Harriet H., p. 19.

HOW MANY DOORS DO YOU OPEN TO RECRUIT A NEW VOLUNTEER

KEEP THE MEMBER INTERESTED AND ON THE JOB
Give him a job that is interesting and important. yet one which will not take more time than he can give.

SIGN ON THE LINE
Get his time commitment and sign up.

SPECIFIC PROPOSAL
Offer him the job of his choice.

CREATE PREFERENCE
List the many volunteer jobs that make up the operation.

AROUSE INTEREST
In the program of your agency in the community.

CONTACT
Find the person you want and find a way to meet him.

RECRUITERS
Must not only know how many people it takes to operate the service, but they also face the necessity of locating all the people who have time and interest to give.

The committee must ferret out and identify the man or woman behind the door or the title who must be called into service. Members of the committee must know the kind of tasks to be performed, the time a volunteer can be expected to give, the time each job will take, and the satisfactions to be gained through service.

TRAINED recruiters and consistent recruiting is the answer to the need to enlist a sufficient number of citizens to carry on the responsibilities of any agency.

Author Unknown

CHAPTER VII

Interviewing and Placing Volunteers

When Confucius was asked the definition of wisdom, his answer was "to know mankind". This answer is as valid today as it was 2500 years ago.

And one of the oldest and most universal methods man has used to assess one another is the interview. One way to know another person is to have a "conversation with a purpose", which is one definition of interviewing.

However, in the field of volunteerism, there are many people who feel very uncomfortable with the concept of utilizing this particiular management tool. They feel it is inappropriate to interview and screen people who are volunteering their services, at least in any but the most casual and superficial fashion.

I firmly disagree with this viewpoint and suggest that we owe it to volunteers to conduct thorough and effective interviews. If we don't, then we are in essence saying to them, "We know what we need and want—but we neither know nor care what you want. Because you are free we have an obligation to accept you". No applicant, whether paid or volunteer, wants to be judged suitable or not for a position without a chance to discuss it face to face.

We also owe it to our agencies and organizations to interview well. When we are about the business of human services we must be responsible about our efforts, or we and our volunteers may do more damage than good.

Ivan Scheier points out that it is necessary to build into our volunteer selection process procedures for ensuring suitability, appropriateness and quality control. We must screen out those clearly unsuited for certain jobs and redirect them to appropriate placements whenever possible. This is essential for several reasons:[1]

1. The clients of the agency must be protected. They must be helped, not hindered by any volunteer involvement;

2. The agency's reputation is greatly affected by the volunteers who work there;

3. Morale of paid staff and other volunteers declines when inappropriate or poor volunteer placements occur; and

4. The volunteer himself suffers when misplaced.

And, just as it is essential to recognize and deal with high risk volunteers, it is just as important to recognize high potential candidates. One of the greatest faults of many volunteer programs is under-utilizing those volunteers who have unusual skills, organizational capabilities or extraordinary potential. These people frequently go undetected because no one interviewed them effectively and once they were placed, they were forgotten.

So for the benefit of all concerned—the agency, volunteer, staff and client—it is important that the task of interviewing and selection be taken seriously.

After six years of working in Personnel Administration in industry and seven years as Director of a volunteer program, I have come to the conclusion that this is one of the least understood and most poorly utilized skills of most managers. There is a strong tendency to view the interview as a friendly chat and to treat it with indifference, or at best, extremely casually. *And yet it will, in my opinion, have a greater impact on the quality of our programs in years to come than any other single factor . . . for it will determine which people will be involved in designing, directing and carrying out those programs. It* is therefore an extremely complex, vital and challenging skill and deserves all of the time and attention we can give to it.

Can everyone become effective interviewers? In my opinion, the answer is no, because interviewing is a strange mixture of acquired skills, certain personal characteristics and an instinct or intuitive sense that some people have and others do not. (Someone once called instinct "the nose of the mind" and as such it is extremely helpful in detecting subtle nuances of meaning in an interview that can be valuable clues to understanding a person.)

In the *Volunteers in Rehabilitation* series, the booklet entitled "How to Interview and Place Volunteers" identifies the qualities they feel are helpful in those who interview volunteers:[2]

1. Ability to converse easily with strangers.
2. Acceptance of all people.
3. Skill in observing or sensing other people's reactions, attitudes, concerns, and personality traits.
4. Ability to listen attentively and hear accurately.
5. Experience as a volunteer.
6. Knowledge of the volunteer jobs in that agency.
7. Ability to speak clearly, and explain things well.
8. Capacity to recognize individual strengths and potential.
9. Experience in working with persons of varied racial, religious, educational and economic backgrounds.
10. Familiarity with the program and the agency or organization.
11. Ability to efficiently guide the conversation without sacrificing sensitivity or purpose.

One of the most interesting, yet difficult things about interviewing is that you must establish almost instant rapport wih a person. In our present "society of strangers," this is not easy. People have become guarded and impersonal in their conversations and frequently have a talent for verbal fencing. Listen to typical cocktail party conversations, neighborhood coffee clatches, or after church or club chatter. People seldom exchange information about much except their activities and mutual associations. Rarely are personal feelings, goals or fears discussed.

The only way I have found to break these barriers, in order to talk about what a person is (not just what he does), is to be genuinely interested in that persons—as a person—and let him or her know it. When it is apparent that you really do care about what he or she needs, wants, and has to offer, real communication begins to take place almost immediately and with it comes the possibility of matching this person to an opening that will be both suitable and satisfying.

When we talk about interviewing skills, two of the most crucial are the ability to ask appropriate questions and the art of listening. Let us examine each of these for a moment.

ASKING QUESTIONS

Have you ever read the delightful children's book, *The Little Prince?* It is one of those deceptively simple, profound stories that encourages several readings. It is a child's view of the adult world and one of the little prince's observations concerns the subject of interviewing in a most interesting and unusual fashion. He says, "Grown-ups love figures. When you tell them you have made a new friend, they never ask any questions about essential matters. They never say to you, 'What does his voice sound like? What games does he love best? Does he collect butterflies?' Instead they demand: 'How old is he? How many brothers has he? How much does he weigh? How much does his father make?' Only from these figures do they think they have learned anything about him."[3]

How many of us who interview fit this description? Frequently, the interview is viewed as the mechanism we must utilize to fill out the blanks on a registration form. Or we may have a well memorized mental questionnaire that we pursue, somehow feeling that if we can only complete that, we will know the person we are interviewing. I would suggest we may know a lot about the person, but I seriously doubt that we know him or her.

It is astounding how the kinds of questions we ask and how we ask them affects what we find out about an applicant.

Consider, for example, the difference in the information you are apt to obtain by these two sets of questions:

I. How old are you?
    Are you married?
    How many children do you have?
    What ages are they?
    What volunteer or paid jobs have you held?

II. Tell me about your family.

What do you most enjoy doing?

What are your personal and work goals that would be important to consider in choosing a volunteer job?

Describe what you would consider to be an ideal job for you, and tell me why?

The first set of questions utilizes the directive approach and I consider it non-productive in most instances. A registration form (such as those included in the Appendix of this Chapter) should give you all of the statistical and pertinent data covered in these questions. By examining the form just prior to the interview, you should be ready to move on to more important areas of inquiry.

The second approach is non-directive, which means the interviewer serves as a skilled catalyst and prober and the applicant becomes the director of the content of what is said.

The following are some suggested kinds of questions that may prove helpful in determining a person's attitudes, values, interpersonal relations, emotional stability and motivations (achievement, power or affiliation). *These questions need to be changed or adapted to your own style and needs, and the particular interview situation.* The important thing they suggest is *how* to phrase questions to enable people to talk about themselves and not keep them from it.

NON-DIRECTIVE INTERVIEWING SUGGESTIONS

1. What have you enjoyed most in previous volunteer assignments? What have you enjoyed least? (ATTITUDES)

2. What kind of people do you work with best as co-workers? What kind of people are you most interested in as clients and why? Are there types of people you feel you'd be unable to work with? (INTERPERSONAL RELATIONS)

3. What would you consider to be the ideal volunteer job for you? Why? (MOTIVATION AND VALUES)

4. What things have you done that have given you greatest satisfaction? (MOTIVATION AND VALUES)

5. Why are you interested in doing volunteer work? What are your long-range objectives? (MOTIVATION)

6. What do you like to do in your leisure time? (VALUES)

7. What is your "energy" or "activity level" and how would you describe your work habits? (WORK HABITS)

8. Thinking back, what are the most significant decisions you have made in your life and how do you feel about them? (DECISION MAKING)

9. What makes you really angry—on the job or at home—and how do you deal with this anger? (EMOTIONAL STABILITY)

10. Tell me about your family. (EMOTIONAL STABILITY)

11. What kind of supervision do you prefer? (MOTIVATION)

12. Describe your temperament. What do you like best about yourself? If you could, what would you improve? (EMOTIONAL STABILITY)

In the *Handbook of Modern Personnel Administration,* it states "the interviewer gets the interviewee to talk freely by asking questions properly, by maintaining silence at appropriate times, and by reflecting or restating what the applicant says to him . . . questions that are based on what the applicant has just said show that the interviewer is listening carefully and encourages the person to continue to talk."[4]

For example, if the volunteer has just identified her favorite volunteer job as that of establishing a tutor program, the next question should be, "tell me how you went about it" and not "tell me about your family."

It might be helpful to examine a report issued by the American Management Association identifying errors most commonly made by interviewers in industry:[5]

1. Asking leading questions;
2. Making decisions too early in the interview;
3. Following a stereotype pattern of interviewing, without recognition of individual differences;
4. Lacking knowledge of precise job requirements;
5. Letting pressure of duties shorten the interview time;
6. Doing more talking than they should;
7. Failing to direct the interview and thereby wasting time;
8. Not knowing what to look for;
9. Tending to be overly influenced by individual factors rather than considering the person as a whole;

126

10. Lacking skill in asking questions and in probing;

11. Failing to describe the job and organization in sufficient detail;

12. Tending to be too routine, instead of adapting each interview to the individual;

13. Being interviewed by the candidate instead of doing the interviewing;

14. Not following up on placements to see if performance bears out the judgment of the interviewer; and

15. The most frequent and difficult to overcome mistake—tending to judge the applicant solely on personality, overlooking other important factors.

It is important to recognize that there are different kinds of interviews and that the purpose of the interview helps to determine both the appropriate format and amount of time required. For our purposes, we will identify the types of interviews as *screening or counseling; in-depth; follow-up or evaluation;* and *exit interviews.*

A. *Screening or Counseling Interview*: This is the initial interview, generally conducted by the person responsible for the entire volunteer program, or by someone delegated this responsibility. The purpose is to determine if the volunteer meets the basic requirements and thus is a suitable candidate for further consideration. It is also important to give the volunteer enough information about the jobs available and the general purpose of the agency so that he might make a decision whether he is interested in your volunteer program, or wishes to look elsewhere.

Many people prefer the term counseling instead of screening, because they view this as an opportunity to counsel the prospective volunteer on available opportunities. The aim is to help the applicant sort through these and at least identify suitable general areas for further consideration, based on goals, time available, interests and skills.

This is also the type of interview conducted most frequently by Volunteer Bureaus and Voluntary Action Centers. Since they recruit for dozens, sometimes hundreds, of different agencies, the goal of the interview is to obtain enough information to make a sensible referral to an appropriate agency. It is then that agency's responsibility to conduct an in-depth interview to determine which client, department and opening is most suitable for this particular volunteer.

It is sometimes helpful in this type of interview to assist the applicant in narrowing choices to two or three possibilities through the process of elimination. By determining what type of job, what kind of client, what age group, how frequent an assignment, etc., the person screens themselves out of many options and the referral can be made accordingly. This interview should require 15-30 minutes in most instances and can be done, *if necessary*, by phone. It is preferable however to have the person come to the office, where, if at all possible, written job descriptions should be available for them to browse through before the interview. We display the jobs from all our agencies in colorful folders on racks in our waiting or browsing room and have found this an invaluable aid in conducting productive, yet concise, initial interviews. And the volunteers enthusiastically appreciate the opportunity to see all of the options themselves.

B. *In-Depth Interview*: As the name implies, this is a more intensive and lengthy interview generally conducted by the person to whom the volunteer will report. Such things as personality traits, skills, likes and dislikes, goals, emotional stability, attitudes and motivation should be explored. The purpose is to obtain enough sound information and personal data to be able to determine if the volunteer is appropriate for a particular position, if she will be a compatible co-worker for other volunteers and paid staff and most especially, if she is to work with a particular client, if they are a suitable match.

Sometimes more than one person interviews the applicant, if it is for a particularly responsible or sensitive position.

The interviewer must be intensely involved in the listening process during this interview or a decision will be made based on inadequate or faulty information. And remember, the volunteer needs to make a decision following this interview as well. We will talk more about listening in a moment.

The time required varies but generally a minimum of 45 minutes to one hour is needed.

C. *Follow-Up or Evaluation Interview*: It is a mistake to think of interviewing as a one-time process. It is vital to have periodic interviews with staff, both paid and volunteer, to evaluate their progress, identify problems and assess promotional possibilities. These can be as formal or informal as you like, as long as they are purposeful and productive and not just a friendly chat and perfunctory "pat on the back" gesture.

D. *Exit Interview*: When a person leaves an organization it is appropriate and helpful to get candid feedback from them. It is valuable to determine why they are leaving and obtain their evaluation of the program. It is also important to encourage their suggestions for improvement.

THE ART OF LISTENING

Listening is more than just not talking. A little boy in a music appreciation class, when asked to distinguish between listening and and hearing replied, "Listening is wanting to hear".

Strauss and Sayles, in *Personnel: The Human Problems of Management,* observe that "listening requires an active effort to convey that you understand and are interested in what the other person is saying—almost that you are helping him say it. A friendly facial expression and an attentive but relaxed attitude are important. A good interviewer also makes use of such phrases as 'Uh-huh,' 'I understand,' 'That explains it,' or 'Could you tell me more?'."[6]

The Handbook of Modern Personnel Administration states, "the essence of non-directive interviewing consists of using silence effectively and of reflecting and restating the ideas of the interviewee. Silence is the interviewer's most powerful tool but reflection and restatement are his sharpest and most incisive."[7]

It has been estimated that the average adult listens with only 25% efficiency, when you define listening as what a person hears, understands and remembers.

Felix M. Lopez points out some pitfalls to effective listening:[8]

1. *Anticipation.* The interviewer frequently anticipates the end of a sentence or statement and instead of continuing to listen, begins to think about the next question.

2. *Intolerance.* When the interviewer is mentally critical of the interviewee due to his speech, appearance or mannerism and thus stops listening. This is where personal prejudice is extremely important to recognize, whether it be race, life-style, length of hair or skirt, or sex. (As the Smothers Brother once said, "No one should be prejudiced against because of the shape of their skin.")

3. *Impulsivity*. Interrupting an applicant's answer to either interject one's own thoughts or to ask another question.

4. *Indolence*. Listening takes such hard mental effort that it is easy to become lazy and let attention wander.

5. *Suggestibility*. Being overly influenced by emotion-laden terms.

Mr. Lopez suggests some aids to being good listeners:

1. *Interest*. The interviewer must consider the interview and applicant to be important and therefore worthy of interest and attention.

2. *Patience*. Rapid-fire interviews are rarely effective. The person must be given time to give thoughtful answers.

3. *Linking*. Build the interview on what the applicant has already said. This is called probing and it indicates to the interviewee that you are listening. It also eliminates the distracting necessity of trying to think up the next question.

4. *Alertness*. Listen for key words and phrases and be sure they are understood.

5. *Concentration*. Listen for main ideas, not just facts and figures. Constantly ask yourself, "What is the applicant telling me?"

6. *Deliberation*. Withhold evaluation and decision until the interview is completed. Hear the person out before deciding.

We have a choice in interviewing as to the philosophical stance we wish to take. Are we primarily concerned with discovering a person's weaknesses or strengths. The cautious interviewer will concentrate on discovering the weaknesses to avoid recommending an unsuitable candidate for a position. But we must realize the opposite error of rejecting a good potential candidate is often worse, because once done, it is irreversible. We must not overlook problems or be unaware of weaknesses, for all people have them. We must, however, counterbalance their impact on our decision by an honest evaluation of the person's strengths and potential. Someone once said, "We have a tendency to judge others only by what they have already done, while we judge ourselves by what we feel capable of doing".

Finally, one cardinal rule in interviewing is *do not keep the applicant dangling*. This is true for both setting up the initial interview and for arriving at and conveying the decision. There is nothing worse for a person than expressing an interest in a job (whether paid or not), then having to wait days or sometimes weeks for someone to call and set up an appointment for an interview. The prospective volunteer reacts with the legitimate observation, "I thought they needed help—I don't believe it!"

And following the interview, the applicant should be clearly informed of the outcome: "I am setting up an appointment for you with the supervisor of the drug clinic;" "We would be very happy to have you join our volunteer program—could you start next week?"; "We are interviewing other candidates this week, but will arrive at a decision by the first of next month and will call you"; or, "I'm sorry, Mr. Jones, it appears your interests and capabilities do not suit our particular volunteer openings at the moment. May I call the Volunteer Bureau and make an appointment for you? They have such a wide variety of opportunities I'm sure you'd find just what you are wanting."

Interviewing is not only challenging—it can be fun. It is an opportunity to really get to know another person, which in my opinion, is one of life's beautiful experiences.

PLACING

Placing the appropriate person in a suitable, well-designed job can be one of the most rewarding experiences of a Director of Volunteers. This is because the greatest challenge and joy for a good manager is not just to produce things . . . but to grow people, and people grow best when given a meaningful job to do that requires the best they have to offer.

This is why the processes of job design and interviewing are so essential, because without either of them, making good placements becomes a matter of sheer luck. To make sensible and imaginative placements involves matching the interests, skills and personal characteristics of the volunteer with the requirements outlined for a specific job. It is like fitting two parts of a puzzle together. When it is the right fit, it helps complete the whole picture of your organization.

Occasionally, however, you will interview a volunteer who has a unique set of skills or unusual potential in a particular area, but you have no job description that fits. You then have a choice of trying to shrink the person to fit an existing job, or to do some exploring with your staff to see if someone would be able to utilize those particular skills in a new and needed project. Many times people do not request certain kinds of volunteer help because it never occurs to them

131

it's possible to obtain it. Some examples might be a researcher, technical librarian graphics artist, interpreter, musician, ecologist, drama coach, etc. It is better to at least attempt to add a new dimension to your program (as long as it legitimately fits and is needed) by utilizing the unique skills of a person, than to ignore those and place them in a traditional volunteer assignment, where their particular contribution will probably not be as great, nor as satisfying to them.

May I give you an example. A volunteer came to our Center several years ago who was an ex-teacher, recently moved to our city. She wanted to volunteer two to four hours a week in the Headstart program. As I interviewed her, it was apparent she was well qualified for that position. However, I also noted an interesting comment on her application form. She stated she had organized a school-aide and tutor program for a suburb of Washington, D.C., as a volunteer. I asked her to tell me about the program and how it had been established. (This was more than idle curiosity, for we had been urged to begin such a program in our city for several months, but did not have enough staff to do so.) As she began to talk about this experience she became so animated and enthusiastic it was apparent it had been a most gratifying accomplishment for her.

As she finished, I saw the possibility of adding a needed dimension to our program. I shared my dilemma with her, asked if she was interested in pursuing the establishment of such a program here and obtained her eager commitment to help me propose it to our Advisory Committee and School Administration. She also stated she would be willing to organize and direct the School Aide and Tutor Task Force for a year if it were formed, again as a volunteer. It was approved and established and because we were able to utilize the unique skills and background of one particular volunteer, between 200-300 elementary school children in our city benefit from volunteer help each year. And yet, it would have been so easy to have placed her at Headstart for 2-4 hours per week.

There are three concerns expressed by volunteers repeatedly:

1. That their volunteer work will be a waste of time;
2. That their skills and talents will not be utilized appropriately; and,
3. That they may be placed in jobs for which they are not suited.

Effective interviewing and placing speaks to all of these concerns and insures that the volunteer's involvement will be meaningful

132

to the agency, as well as a satisfying, growing experience for the volunteer.

Voltaire, in his book *Zadig, A Mystery of Fate*, asks the following question:

"What, of all things in the world, is the longest and the shortest, the swiftest and the slowest, the most divisible and the most extended, the most neglected and the most regretted, without which nothing can be done, which devours all that is little, and enlivens all that is great?"

And Zadig answered:

"Time."

"Nothing is longer, since it is the measure of eternity.

"Nothing is shorter, since it is insufficient for the accomplishment of your projects.

"Nothing is more slow to him that expects, nothing more rapid to him that enjoys.

"In greatness it extends to infinity, in smallness it is infinitely divisible.

"All men neglect it; all regret the loss of it; nothing can be done without it.

"It consigns to oblivion whatever is unworthy of being transmitted to posterity, and it immortalizes such actions as are truly great.

Time is man's most precious asset."[9]

And since *time* is what the volunteers are offering, it is essential that we take them and their offer seriously.

References

1. Scheier, Ivan H., *Using Volunteers In Court Settings*, U. S. Dept. of Health, Education and Welfare, J. D. Publication, No. 477, p. 46.

2. Levin, Stanley, *Volunteers in Rehabilitation Series*: "How to Interview and Place Volunteers," Goodwill Industries, 1973, p. 4.

3. Exupéry, Antoine de Saint, *The Little Prince*, Harcourt Brace Jovanovich, Inc. 1943-71, p. 16.

4. Famularo, Joseph L., *Handbook of Modern Personnel Administration*, McGraw-Hill Book Co., 1972, p. 13-8.

5. American Management Study 47, "The Employment Interview."

6. Strauss, George and Sayles, Leonard R., *Personnel: The Human Problems of Management*, Prentice-Hall, Inc., 1972, p. 232.

7. Famularo, Joseph L., p. 13-8.

8. Famularo, Joseph L., p. 13-9 & 10.

9. Quoted in *The Public Speakers' Treasure Chest*, Prochnow, Herbert V., Harper & Row, 1964, p. 296.

Volunteer and Information Center of Boulder County
2305 Canyon Blvd., Boulder, Colo.
444-4904

VOLUNTEER REGISTRATION FORM

The information on this form will help us to find the most satisfying and appropriate volunteer service for you. Your cooperation in completing it is most appreciated.

Name _____ Date _____
      First   Middle   Last (please print)

Home address: _____ Home Telephone: _____

_____ Work Telephone: _____
    City   State

Date of Birth: _____No. of Children_____Ages_____

Education (circle last yr. completed)   Grade 5 6 7 8   High School 1 2 3 4

                                    College 1 2 3 4   Graduate 1 2 3 4

Previous work experience: _____

Are you presently employed: Yes _____ No _____If yes, hours per wk. _____

Your duties in this job: _____

Employer's name and address: _____

Special skills, training, interests or hobbies (crafts, music, drama, etc): _____
_____

_____

Previous or present volunteer jobs: _____

What kinds of volunteer jobs are you most interested in at present? _____

Do you prefer any particular age group or type of client, if not covered above: _____

Time you have available for volunteer work:

Hours per week_____ Regularly each week: Yes_____No_____

Almost anytime: Yes_____ No _____

Any preferred days and hours? _____

Do you have a car with adequate insurance and would you be willing to drive it to transport clients as part of your volunteer work? Yes _____No _____Uncertain_____. We would be interested in any further comments or information you might wish to offer: _____
_____
_____

FOR OFFICE USE ONLY

Date of Interview: _____ Interviewed by: _____

Volunteer's preferences: _____

     1. _____

     2. _____

     3. _____

     4. _____

Comments: _____

_____

_____

Source of Referral to VIC: _____

_____

Assignments: _____ Date _____

     1. _____ Date _____

     2. _____ Date _____

     3. _____ Date _____

     4. _____ Date _____

     5. _____ Date _____

     6. _____ Date _____

Follow up on placements: _____

_____

_____

_____

_____

_____

_____

136

INTEREST AND HOBBY CHECKLIST FOR VOLUNTEERS

An informal checklist such as the one following will assist the new recruit in clarifying his or her own interests in relation to the job. The checklist can be a device used for a first conversation between the volunteer and recruiter or mailed as a follow-up to a meeting.

Groups or individuals can use the checklist and, if desired, it may be modified or adapted according to the needs of the particular group or organization.

What I Like to Do	All the Time	Most of the Time	A Little	Not at All	Comment
Reading and writing					
Taking responsibility					
Speaking to groups					
Meeting new people					
Dancing and singing					
Sorting papers, keeping records					
Typing					
Fixing machines					
Drawing and sketching					
Camping, living out-of-doors					
Research and analysis					
Swimming and hiking					
Working "math" problems					
Selling or contacting people					
Experimenting with mechanical devices					
Making things; repairing					
Teaching					
Cooking and entertaining					
Designing clothes and decorating					
Making decisions					
Presiding at meetings and events					
Acting in a play					
Directing a dramatic production					
Leading a discussion group					
Driving a car					

Other (list or describe here):

Anne K. Stenzel and Helen M. Feeney, *Volunteer Training & Development: A Manual for Community Groups*, New York: Seabury Press, 1968, p. 94-95.

CHAPTER VIII

Training: Designing Creative Learning Experiences

For many people, the term "training" conjures up images of a very particular and restricted sort of learning situation. Dogs are trained to hunt, sit, heel and be obedient. Factory workers are trained to run machines and punch time clocks. Babies are toilet trained, and so on.

It is extremely important for our purposes in this book that we view training from a very different perspective. Training is meant to encompass anything that helps to increase the realization of a person's or organization's potential.

Another term used by behavioral scientists for training is *human resource development* and it is defined as "focusing on the broad developmental process of people as resources to themselves, groups, organizations, communities, and larger cultures . . . it is by no means a luxury; it is the key to unlock creative helping and problem-solving processes that can move a changing society forward."[1]

Viewed from this perspective it becomes immediately apparent why those of us in the field of volunteer administration need to understand and utilize training effectively.

The intent of this Chapter is not to offer the reader packaged training models, for the diversity and flexibility of this field would make this impractical and, in my opinion, short-sighted. Instead we will examine some basic philosophies and theories about adult learning, explore those factors and methods that have relevance to most learning situations and suggest particular areas where they might be applied in volunteer programs. The actual application to individual training problems within your own organization is a challenge that can best be met by you.

Let us begin by looking at the educational system, then move on to the phenomenon of learning. This will then lead us directly into training, as one avenue or vehicle of the learning process.

A noted expert in the field of education, Warren Bennis, states, "Our educational system should (1) help us to identify with the adaptive process without fear of losing our identity; (2) increase tolerance of ambiguity without fear of losing intellectual mastery; (3) increase our ability to collaborate without fear of losing our individuality; and, (4) develop a willingness to participate in social evolution while recognizing implacable forces. In short, we need an educational system that can help make a virtue out of contingency rather than one which induces hesitancy or its reckless companion, expedience."[2]

There is, to my way of thinking, no field that more desperately needs this kind of educational climate than volunteerism. How frequently do we decide by not deciding, or act out of a sense of inadequacy or expediency due to finding ourselves on the unchartered waters of constant societal changes. Community problems and needs change, bringing with them necessary changes in human service programs. The volunteer work forces in these programs are also in a perpetual state of flux. Therefore it becomes essential that we develop both as persons and as professionals to be able to deal creatively with ambiguity and contingency, not be defeated by them.

As Sydney Harris, the columnist once wrote, our dilemma is that we hate change and love it at the same time; what we really want is for things to remain the same, but get better.

But rationally we know things won't get better in our communities unless we invest ourselves, as individuals and as organizations, in a clear and decisive plan to unlock human resources. The strengths, talents and ingenuity that made this country great are still there, in every community, but somehow we have forgotten how to effectively unleash them. Perhaps human resource development may be one answer.

Let us consider the hopeful outcome of education . . . learning. (Note, I say hopeful). Learning is a very complex process. It happens within a person, not to them and involves the mind, emotions, values, interests, and, ideally, behavior. As such it is a very personal and individual process. This is frequently overlooked in our efforts to communicate to and educate the masses.

The old transmittal theory, that education is a process of transmitting the totality of human knowledge from one generation to the next, has become both obsolete and impossible in light of today's knowledge explosion. John Ingalls suggests, "Perhaps our purpose could be to stimulate in the learner a desire to engage in a lifelong process of discovering what he needs to know. Education, as a lifelong process of continuing discovery and growth, could satisfy our need to relate in a positive and personal way to our own changing experience."[3]

The Japanese have already incorporated this concept into their industrial institutions. Peter Drucker found that continuous learning is an integral part of successful Japanese businesses today. Every employee, often up to and including top managers, keeps on training as a regular part of his job until he retires. According to Drucker, this creates receptivity for the new, the different, the innovative, the more productive. The focus in the training sessions is always on doing the job better, doing it differently, doing it in new ways.[4] This would seem to be one effective means of preventing the apathy and boredom so destructively present in many organizations.

It illustrates the Zen approach to learning, which regards the purpose of learning as self-improvement or the ability to do one's present job with continually wider vision and increased competence and with continually rising demands on oneself.

In an article in *Optimizing Human Resources*, Leslie This and Gordon Lippitt identify five basic kinds of learning:[5]

1. Knowing something intellectually or conceptually one never knew before.

2. Being able to do something one couldn't do before—behavior or skill.

3. Combining two knowns into a new understanding of a skill, piece of knowledge, concept or behavior.

141

4. Being able to use or apply a new combination of skills, knowledge, concept or behavior.

5. Being able to understand, and/or apply that which one knows—either skill, knowledge, or behavior.

And Harriet Naylor suggests "layers of learning" can be identified:[6]

Unawareness: Couldn't care less
↓
Awareness: Notice, but wonder if true
↓
Interest: Think it might be important
↓
Acceptance: Tested against experience, seems to be true
↓
Conviction: Important to me and others
↓
Commitment: Overriding importance to me—determines how I feel and act

It is when the learning experience of those involved in our volunteer programs reaches the commitment and conviction levels that we have achieved our goal. But Douglas McGregor warns, "knowledge cannot be pumped into human beings the way grease is forced into a fitting on a machine. The individual may learn; he is not taught. Effective education is always a process of influence by integration and self-control."[7]

And this, then, is the challenge of a trainer—to assist others in their process of "becoming." To do this, we must ourselves be constantly engaged in the exciting pursuit of new learnings and insights. We must, at all costs, avoid "tunnel vision" and be receptive to what we can learn through our own experience and the experiences of others. The trainer must infect others with his or her contagious enthusiasm for learning.

One of the aspects of learning that is gaining more and more attention is the differences between child learning (pedogogy) and adult learning (andragogy). Until recent years, most studies conducted about learning were based on learning in children and animals, and most of what was known about teaching related to child learning

142

experiences. That is why so much adult education has been less than successful, for adults were being taught as though they were children.

One of the most interesting and informative efforts in this area was done by Data Education, Inc., of Waltham, Massachusetts, under a contract from the Social and Rehabilitation Service of the U.S. Department of Health, Education and Welfare in 1973. They produced *A Trainer's Guide to Andragogy* by John D. Ingalls.

In this manual, Dr. Malcom Knowles, author of *The Modern Practice of Adult Education*, identifies four basic concepts that illustrate the differences in adult and child learning experiences:[8]

1. *Difference in Self-Concept*:

    As a person moves from childhood to adulthood, their self-concept normally changes from dependency to independence or self-direction. They, therefore, resent being placed in learning situations where they are treated as children (told what to do, talked down to, judged, etc.). This clearly indicates the best learning climate for adults is one of mutual respect between leader and learner, and where the role of leader is supportive not directive. The students should be encouraged to determine their own learning needs and take part in the planning and evaluating of the learning experience. Their concept of being responsible and self-directed should be encouraged, not violated. [This would seem to be worth utilizing with young people as well, in my opinion.]

2. *Difference in Accumulated Experience.*

    By the simple process of living longer, adults have acquired a vastly larger and more varied store of experiences than children. These experiences make the adult learner a potentially rich resource to be utilized in the learning experience. This also provides adults with a broader foundation of past experiences on which new learnings can be built, if the relationship between "new" and "old" can be appropriately illustrated. This is why, in andragogy, it is essential to utilize two-way learning modes, where students are both learners and teachers, i.e., group discussions, role play, buzz groups, task groups, skills practice sessions.

3. *Difference in Readiness to Learn.*

    Determining the "teachable moment" is a constant challenge for the teacher or trainer, whether the student is adult or child.

143

In pedagogy, the teacher has traditionally taken the responsibility of determining both what a child will learn and what sequence learning should follow. Dr. Knowles urges that with adults the sequence of learnings should be strongly influenced by the developmental tasks and needs of the learners (which they themselves identify), rather than simply by the logic of the subject matter or the needs of the organization.

4. *Difference in Time Perspective.*

Youth usually think of education as future oriented—what will I need to know when I get a job, become a parent, etc. Adults, however, approach education from the standpoint of "doing in the present"—of being able to utilize and apply the learning immediately. This necessitates a shift from subject centered to problem centered educational experiences in most adult training. The goal is to discover "where are we now" and "where do we want to go" and to design adult learning experiences to close that gap.

Dr. Knowles concludes, "The truly artistic teacher of adults perceives the focus of responsibility for learning to be in the learner; he conscientiously suppresses his own compulsion to teach what he knows his students ought to learn in favor of helping his students learn for themselves what they want to learn."[9]

One of the dilemmas of training is that it is so easy either to neglect it entirely, or to use it inappropriately (assuming that it is a sort of magic cure-all for anything that ails us). One of the obvious reasons for training both volunteers and staffs is to improve performance. But in a delightful book entitled *Analyzing Performance Problems or You Really Oughta Wanna,* the authors point out that training is not always the answer to performance problems.

"Sometimes the solution is to provide information; if he doesn't know, instruction is likely to help. But when a person does know how and still doesn't perform, you can teach and exhort until your socks fall off and not solve the problem. Until the problem is understood, proposing a solution is simply shooting from the hip."[10] Some questions we need to ask ourselves are:

1) What is the difference between what is being done and what is supposed to be done?

2) Is this difference really important (or a matter of . . . "but we've always done it this way")?

3) Does the volunteer possess the necessary skills to do the job —and if not, can he or she learn them?

4) If the skills can be learned, how is the best way to teach them?

5) Is there a more sensible way of doing the job—(does the job rather than the performance need to be changed)?

6) Are there obstacles to good performance that need to be considered; lack of time or tools; unclear definition of duties or instruction; uncomfortable or inappropriate environment, restrictive or oppressive organizational climate?

7) What are all alternative solutions (instruction; remove obstacles; transfer volunteer; change procedures; improve climate . . . or training)? Choose the most sensible solution for that particular situation. It may even be "do nothing".

Assuming your decision at the end of this exercise is that you do, in fact, have a training problem, the next question is what kind of training is in order? Some choices you have are pre-job training, on-the-job training or continuing education. Each is suitable for both staff and volunteers in particular situations.

Pre-Job Training. As the name implies, this is training designed to prepare a person for a particular job before he or she begins. It may include reading appropriate handbooks and material; seeing films; attending lectures; observing others doing the job; learning about the organization, its clients, goals, structure, policies and procedures. (This is often called orientation.)

On-the-Job Training. This provides the learner with the opportunity to extend knowledge, improve skills, and perfect performance by such means as one-to-one instruction, group sessions, role play, or skills workshops conducted while the person is performing the job.

Continuing Education. Learning should be a lifelong process and therefore human resources development should continue to provide the possibilities for all persons in the organization to develop to their fullest potential. This is as important for volunteers as it is for paid staff. Seminars, workshops, adult education classes, university extension courses, management training, all provide opportunities for growth if they are done well.

145

There are certain basic elements relating to structure or climate that need to be considered in any training situation. The *Trainers Guide to Andragogy* suggests the following list to review any time you are planning an adult learning session.[11]

A CLIMATE SETTING CHECKLIST

Physical Surroundings	Human and Interpersonal Relations	Organizational
Space	Welcoming	Policy
Lighting	Comfort Setting	Structure
Acoustics/Outside Noise	Informality	Clientele
Decor	Warm-up Exercise	Policy and Structure
Temperature	Democratic Leadership	Committee
Ventilation	Interpersonal Relations	Meeting Announcements
Seating: Comfort/Position	Handling VIPs	Informational Literature
Seating Arrangements:	Mutual Planning	Program Theme
Grouping/Mobility/	Assessing Needs	Advertising
Rest/Change	Formulating Objectives	Poster, Displays
Refreshments	Designing and Implementing	Exhibits
Writing Materials	Activities	Budget and Finance
Ash Trays	Evaluating	Publish Agenda and
Rest Rooms	Closing Exercise	Closing Time
Audiovisual Aids (including	Close on Time (Option	Frequency of Scheduling
extension cords and out-	to Stay)	Meetings
lets)		
Coat Racks		
Parking		
Traffic Directions		
Records/Addresses, etc.		
Name Tags or Cards		

It is astounding what a negative effect these factors can have on participants if they are overlooked or handled poorly. They illustrate so well Herzberg's "hygiene factors"—they do not in themselves motivate, but if neglected, they can certainly act as *de-motivators* Let me illustrate:

I have conducted training sessions when the air conditioning failed in mid-July or where the room divider in the meeting area did not filter out the noise of an adjoining group. The effect on the learners was disastrous (and on me as well).

Or, another example might be provided by our last conference at the University of Colorado. We furnished free shuttle service, morning and afternoon between the conference area, dorms and parking lots (a 5-7 block route). No one commented on the evaluations that the shuttle service made a positive contribution to the conference's success (in fact, it was never mentioned), but I am almost certain that had it been missing, many negative comments would have appeared and we would have had irritated participants each morning.

The opposite is true of the other two examples—on the evaluations of those sessions, the lack of air conditioning and the noise level were mentioned repeatedly and affected the overall success of the sessions.

And may I strongly suggest that many of these arrangements and details be delegated to someone other than the person responsible for the training content and faculty. At our Center (VIC), we have a special Task Force to assist staff with all training events and they are responsible for all such matters. At the University, the Bureau of Conferences and Institutes handles all arrangements and physical aspects of the conferences (which they do expertly) and I am free, as faculty director, to deal only with content, methods and faculty.

Perhaps it would be helpful to attempt to diagram a sequence of steps one should follow in planning most kinds of training:

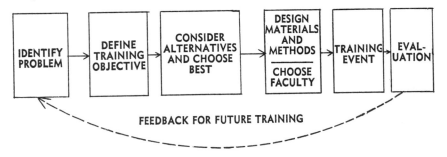

It is important to involve everyone who will be involved, or affected by the training in this whole process. Naturally, not all trainees can attend planning meetings, but their input can be secured through questionnaires, evaluations of past training events, interviews, and at least a sample representation on the planning committee.

After the objectives and content of a workshop or learning experience have been determined, it is important to examine the rich array of methods and formats available to decide how the content can most effectively be presented to achieve the desired objective. Variety and creativity should be generously utilized. This is where the fun of planning a training event lies.

One of the first decisions concerns size and composition of the learning group for each session: Some choices are:

Convention
Large general sessions (plenary)

Conference
Skills Workshops
Small Group Discussions/Problem Solving
Task Groups
Courses
Individual Study
One-to-One Instruction

Some of the methods that can be utilized in some or all of these formats would be:

Lecturettes/Lectures
Role Play
Groups
Audio-visuals—
   Movies
   Slides
   Overhead Projector
   Film Strips
   Records/Tape
   Cassettes
   Video Tape
   Flip Chart
   Posters
   Charts
   Graphs
   Flannel Board
   Chalk Board
Panel Discussions
Demonstrations
Tours or Trips
Exhibits
Team Teaching
Brainstorming
Case Study
Simulation Games
Observation
Dramatization

The final crucial decision to be made in each training situation is who should do it. The choice of faculty or trainers is a critical one for they determine the outcome of the venture. Here again, we have a vast reservoir of talent in any community to draw from. Some

148

suggestions might be: professional staff from your agency, clients (most useful, but most frequently overlooked), volunteers, management specialists from industry, directors of successful volunteer programs, faculty from community colleges and universities, outside consultants, agency executives, businessmen. Once again seek out the particular experience or expertise you need—but *be sure* the person you choose cares about volunteerism, listens and responds to the group, tailors what is presented to your needs (not theirs) and is a warm and reachable type of learner/teacher.

The Goodwill series booklet entitled "How to Prepare Volunteers to Help"[12] gives helpful suggestions about implementing some of these methods in specific kinds of volunteer training, as does the Jorgensen and Scheier book *Volunteer Training For Courts and Corrections.*[13]

The process of planning for a training event like all other planning, should include evaluation from the very beginning. The more clearly the goals and objectives of the training are articulated the more easily it can be effectively evaluated. You either did or did not accomplish what you set out to accomplish and when you determine this, then you can decide what factors contributed to the success or failure and incorporate what was learned into future training efforts.

At a recent conference I attended in Maine, Marvin Arffa, the founding Editor/Publisher of *Volunteer Administration,* presented some helpful questions we need to deal with as we design training programs and evaluations:

1. What is the need?
2. What do we want to accomplish? (State objectives)
3. Who are to be trained? (Identify professional or nonprofessional persons or other classifications)
4. How many are to be trained?
5. What is the present general level of knowledge and experience of those to be trained?
6. What are the general capabilities of those to be trained?
7. What new knowledge and understanding will be required? (Outline the general scope and content of instructions)
8. What new or improved skills will be needed? (Indicate behavior goals)
9. How can the training or development be conducted? (Consider appropriate methodology and plan of operation)

10. What instructional materials and aids are available or obtainable?
11. What time factors need to be considered? (Include availability of trainees, work requirements, personal needs of trainees, on whose time are they going to be trained, and travel considerations)
12. What should be the starting date, timing, frequency, and length of sessions?
13. What should be the content and sequence of the sessions?
14. Who is to do the training?
15. Is instructor training needed?
16. If so, what training is needed?
17. What instructor guides or lesson plans are needed, and what information should those guides or lesson plans contain?
18. Where is the program to be conducted?
19. What facilities, equipment and services will be required?
20. What study or instructional materials will be used?
21. What records and reports will be needed?
22. How will participants be selected?
23. How will participants be prepared for the learning experience?
24. What will be the estimated cost of the program? (These would be itemized according to personnel, materials, and supplies)
25. How will results of training be measured and evaluated?

And after training, it is helpful to know:

—Emotional reactions and feelings of trainees;
—Information received—what was useful and significant, what clear or unclear, what of little or no value;
—Effectiveness of trainers and group processes utilized;
—Suggestions for future sessions and general comments.

Once again, the actual format of the evaluative instrument will vary depending on the group being evaluated, type of training event, etc. Some sample evaluation or reaction forms are included at the end of this Chapter.

The Director of Volunteers has several very specific training situations to consider: 1) training volunteers; 2) training staff to work effectively with volunteers; 3) team building; and 4) self development. Let us consider each briefly.

Training Volunteers: One of the responsibilities Directors have is to equip volunteers with the basic skills and knowledge they need to perform their volunteer assignments effectively. Orientation should be planned to acquaint each volunteer with the organization and its goals, the people with whom he or she will work (both staff and clients), the task itself and its significance to the whole, and any other information that the volunteer indicates would be helpful. Staff, clients and other volunteers should be incorporated into this learning experience.

Unfortunately, many agencies feel orientation is the only type of training that needs to be provided for volunteers. As we have indicated earlier, that is only the beginning. The volunteers who have ongoing learning opportunities both extend and deepen their contribution to the program. This should not only be allowed, but encouraged. Remember—growing people is the greatest challenge for a manager.

To determine what kinds of continuous learning might be appropriate for your volunteers—*ask them.* They may want skills workshops (to learn to interview, write news releases, make slide presentations, train other volunteers, etc.), or they may want to do outside reading, attend lectures, take part in appropriate staff meetings. Our task is to make learning opportunities available, worthwhile and enjoyable.

There are several general observations we might make about most volunteer training:

1. It is important to understand and appreciate the skills and experiences volunteers bring with them. In line with andragogy, we should utilize these experiences to enrich the learning process by using group process, problem solving techniques, role plays and also by having present volunteers become trainers for future volunteers.

2. Since adults learn for the present, as opposed to the future, the training should be practical versus theoretical and designed to help them do their volunteer jobs better tomorrow.

3. Volunteer training should be relevant, rewarding, informal, and on-going.

4. Time required for training should be realistic and take into consideration that volunteers have many other commitments. The amount of training required should be directly related to the complexity of the job to be done. (An errand runner does not need the same depth of training as a hot line counselor.)

5. Training sessions can also be fruitfully utilized as a reward and/or preparation for promotion to a more responsible volunteer assignment. When sessions are offered to the paid staff such as "Death & Dying", "Interviewing Techniques", "Behavior Modification", "Reality Orientation"—interested volunteers could greatly benefit from being invited to participate and would undoubtedly regard it as a real growth opportunity.

Training Staff To Work With Volunteers: One of the primary reasons for either the slow decay or quick demise of many volunteer programs is lack of staff acceptance and support. Volunteers can only work effectively as part of a team. The other part of that team is paid staff. If volunteers are rejected as legitimate co-workers, both morale and performance suffers irreparably.

Perhaps the most effective way to deal with this situation is to anticipate it and hopefully minimize it by including staff in the entire planning, implementing and evaluating process of the volunteer program.

If you are just beginning to use volunteers, or are adding a dimension to your existing program, include appropriate and affected staff members before, not after the fact. Planning sessions can serve very effectively as training opportunities. Have staff articulate their concerns and needs and deal with them then, as a group. Those who have had good experiences in the past in using volunteers (or being volunteers) should be encouraged to share at this time. It is essential that staff feel a sense of ownership of the volunteer program—that it is theirs, not yours.

By incorporating effective films, slide presentations, presentations by staff and volunteers of other agencies or departments, group discussion sessions, role play or simulation games, staff can become comfortable with the idea of volunteers as a potential help, not threat. Those who still do not accept the concept of volunteer co-workers should definitely not be forced to accept them. It is unfair to all concerned, especially the client or consumer. Remember, a good volunteer job is one which makes sense to volunteers, staff and client!

If you have a volunteer program that has been in existence for sometime, that is becoming stagnant or decreasing in effectiveness, once again the first priority is to determine the problem (remember, "You Really Oughta Wanna"). Perhaps you do have a training problem. If so, it can best be identified by those affected by the program —staff, volunteers and clients. The sensible thing to do is ask their help (through group meetings, questionnaires, interviews) and involve them not only in identifying the problem, but in determining and implementing the solution. Again, role play, dramatization, task groups, problem solving sessions, brainstorming and other experiential formats are usually effective.

Team Building: The situation just described illustrates one important aspect of team building, where staff and volunteers are enabled to work out difficulties and form more satisfying and productive partnerships.

Another type of team building that is essential for a Director of Volunteers to consider is his or her own team of co-workers and subordinates. How effectively does the Office of Volunteers function; are there staff and volunteer differences; does the team and each individual on it have clearly identified and articulated goals and objectives that are compatible; are subordinates encouraged to participate in training events, take courses, read and explore all possible growth opportunities; does anyone feel "locked in" and if so, what is being done about it; and finally, how does staff and your Board or Advisory Committee relate.

Training tools to be used here are individual and group meetings, retreats, mutual goal setting/problem solving sessions, outside consultants, skills workshops, courses, seminars. Do not forget to include staff training in your budget.

I have utilized the instrument included in Chapter IV, Profile of Volunteer/Staff Characteristics", as a basis for both problem solving and goal setting with my paid staff, volunteers and Advisory Committee as a group. We each completed the form and turned it in before the session so it could be analyzed and the results made available to the group. The day was spent struggling with the gaps between where we were as a group and where we wanted to be. We ended up identifying 12 priorities for the year and then appointed sub-groups of staff and volunteers to help determine plans of implementation for each. It was a tremendous experience of team building.

A question any manager must constantly ask himself or herself is "Can my group function well without me?" It appears on the surface to be a rather suicidal question—for if they can get along without you, then maybe they don't need you at all (and what will happen when the boss or board finds out?). Actually, it is the way to determine if you have built a team or an empire. Robert Townsend calls some institutions "monuments to an ego instead of centers of conviction". A good team can compensate and adjust to the temporary loss of a member, even the manager.

In fact, there is a story about Andrew Carnegie that claims he sent his top managers on periodic 6 months leaves of absence. He would tell them before they left, "If your department is in better shape when you get back than when you left, you get a raise. If it falls apart, you are fired".

Are we team building? If not, why not? In training, as in everything else, the climate of the organization and your own management style are crucial factors in determining the success or failure of the endeavor.

Self-Development. One of the most effective ways to create a climate which encourages continuous learning is to engage in it yourself. Drucker points out that managers are made, not born. Therefore, the individual manager needs development as much as a company or society does. "He [or she] should keep alert and mentally alive . . . keep challenged. He must acquire today skills which will make him *effective* tomorrow. He also needs an opportunity to reflect on the meaning of his own experience and above all, he needs an opportunity to reflect on himself and to learn to make his strengths count. He needs development as a person even more than development as a manager."[14]

If we can set for ourselves a goal of continuing growth and development and never cease to cherish the joy and satisfaction that comes from self-discovery and increasing awareness of the world around us, then complacency will never be a problem.

Sometimes it is useful to engage in a disciplined program of self-development. We must first determine which knowledge, insights or understanding, attitudes or skills we wish to develop and then determine how that might best be accomplished. If we believe in the concepts of adult education as they apply to others, we must also apply them to ourselves. We know what we need and want to learn

154

better than anyone else. It is up to us to take the responsibility for our own development.

Until recently, opportunity for training in the field of volunteer administration has been very limited. This is changing rapidly. It is crucial that those of us engaged in the field join forces with academia to help define and implement more and better training opportunities. Hopefully, we will soon be able to offer a rich array of choice for both those presently engaged in volunteer administration and those preparing to enter it. Academic degrees, certification programs, seminars and workshops, and correspondence courses all have their place in raising the standards and level of competency in this vital work.

Finally, whether we approach training as a trainer or trainee, it is important to recognize the essential ingredients of a good adult learning experience, as outlined by James Jorgensen: openness; mutual trust; mutual respect; mutual concern; challenge; and excitement.

Our purpose in training should be to extend horizons, encourage competency, build confidence, and finally to share the exhilaration of new discovery.

References

1. Lippitt, Gordon L., This, Leslie E., and Bidwell, Robert G. Jr., *Optimizing Human Resources*, Addison-Wesley Pub. Co., 1971, Preface & p. 1.

2. Ibid, p. 30. Quoted from a paper presented by Bennis at a meeting of the American Psychological Assoc., Los Angeles, Sept. 4, 1964.

3. Ingalls, John D., *A Trainer's Guide to Andragogy*, Superintendent of Documents, U. S. Government Printing Office, Washington D.C. 20402, p. 2.

4. Drucker, Peter F., *Management: Tasks, Responsibilities, Practices,* Harper and Row, 1973-74, p. 248.

5. Lippitt, This and Bidwell, p. 41. Quoted from Training & Development Journal, 20, Nos. 4 & 5 (April & May, 1966).

6. Naylor, Harriet H., *Volunteers Today: Finding, Training and Working With Them,* Dryden Assoc., 1967-73, p. 111.

7. McGregor, Douglas, *The Human Side of Enterprise,* McGraw-Hill, 1960, p. 211.

8. Ingalls, pp. 4-6.

9. Ibid, p. 24.

10. Mager, Robert F. and Pipe, Peter, *Analyzing Performance Problems,* Fearon Publishers, 1970, p. 2.

11. Ingalls, p. 19.

12. Levin, Stanley, *Volunteers in Rehabilitation Series,* Goodwill Industries of America, Inc., 1973.

13. Jorgensen, James D. and Scheier, Ivan H., *Volunteer Training For Courts and Corrections,* The Scarecrow Press, Inc., 1973.

14. Drucker, p. 421.

Sample Form A

DAILY QUESTIONNAIRE*

Potential Fulfillment Rehabilitation Center
Everycity, Everystate

EVALUATION OF TODAY'S PROGRAM

Date of Program _____

1. How would you rate today's program on an overall basis?

   _____ Excellent   _____ Poor
   _____ Good   _____ Not worthwhile
   _____ Fair   _____ Other (please specify)

2. Which session(s) or part(s) of today's program do you feel was (were) the most worthwhile?
   Why?

3. Which session(s) or part(s) of today's program do you feel was (were) the least worthwhile?

4. Did today's program add to your knowledge and/or skills?
   _____ Yes _____ How?
   _____ No   _____ Why not?

5. Did today's program help prepare you to perform your volunteer duties and responsibilities?
   _____ Yes _____ How?
   _____ No   _____ Why not?

6. Could today's program be improved?   _____ Yes _____ No

7. How would you rate the chief leader of today's program?
   _____ Excellent _____ Fair _____ Unsatisfactory

8. How would you rate the participation of any special speakers or resource persons who were involved in today's program?
   Specifically:

(OPTIONAL)   Name of Trainee_____

                   Date_____

*From Goodwill Industries Series Booklet: "How to Prepare Volunteers to Help."

Sample Form B

CONCLUDING QUESTIONNAIRE*

Potential Fulfillment Rehabilitation Center
Everycity, Everystate

EVALUATION OF TOTAL LEARNING/TRAINING PROGRAM

Date(s) of Program_____

1. On an overall basis how would you rate this program?
   (Check one)

   _____Excellent   _____Poor

   _____Good   _____Not worthwhile

   _____Fair   _____Other (please specify)

2. In terms of quality, RANK the different sessions of this program.
   (E for Excellent, G for Good, F for Fair, P for Poor)
   _____Operation and Program of this Facility
   _____Needs and Problems of Handicapped Persons
   _____The Rehabilitation Process
   _____Role of the Volunteer Program
   _____Community Relationships
   _____Definition of Terms
   _____Important Policies and Regulations

3. Which of your own expectations of this program were fulfilled?

   _____

   _____

4. Which of your own expectations of this program were not fulfilled?

   _____

   _____

   _____

5. What information or skill(s) gained through this program is (are) most valuable to you?

   _____

   _____

6. What suggestions do you have for future programs of this nature?
   a. Number of sessions_____
   b. Length of each session_____
   c. Subjects to be covered_____
   d. Methods to be used_____
   e. Other_____

(OPTIONAL) Name of Trainee _____

                Date_____

*From Goodwill Industries Series: "How to Prepare Volunteer Help."

APPENDIX C

PARTICIPANT REACTION FORM*

PROGRAM: _____ Date: _____

We would appreciate your sharing with us your feelings and reactions to this program so that we can evaluate it and, where appropriate, make changes to improve its usefulness. Please answer the questions below as frankly as possible and use the "comments" spaces provided for any additional thoughts or suggestions you may have.

1. Overall, how would you rate this program in terms of its value to you?
   (Please circle one number reflecting your feeling.)

1	2	3	4	5	6	7	8	9
Poor		Fair		Average		Good		Excellent

2. For each of the items below, please place an X in the appropriate column.

	Excellent	Good	Average	Fair	Poor
a) How well was the program content organized?	——	——	——	——	——
b) How well was the material presented by the instructor?	——	——	——	——	——
c) How well did the instructor keep your interest?	——	——	——	——	——
d) How well did the instructor respond to questions or issues raised by participants?	——	——	——	——	——
e) How did you feel about the physical facilities (e.g., conference room, furniture, etc.)?	——	——	——	——	——

COMMENTS:

EXHIBIT I

*From *Handbook of Modern Personnel Administration*, by Joseph Famularo, published by McGraw Hill, 1972.

END OF SESSION REACTION FORM
VIC "How To" Workshop for Agencies

1. Did you find this workshop meaningful?

(a) Very Much( )	(b) Quite a Bit ( )	(c) Some, but not much ( )	(d) Very Little ( )

2. Did you learn any new facts or get any new ideas that would be helpful on your job?

Certainly did ( )	Probably did ( )	Maybe ( )	Not at all ( )

3. Was there enough opportunity for participation?

Too Much ( )	All that was needed ( )	Should have been more ( )	Should have been much more ( )

4. What did you like best about this workshop?

5. What suggestions do you have for future workshops (content, techniques, materials, tempo, etc.)?

CHAPTER IX

Communications:
Meaning or Message

"A word is not a crystal, transparent and unchanging; it is the skin of a living thought and may vary greatly in color and content according to the circumstances and time in which it is used."

Oliver Wendell Holmes

"Effective communication is the lubricant that can prevent friction between human beings."

Alfred Fleishman

"True listening builds strength in other people."

Robert Greenleaf

"If I can listen to what he can tell me, if I can understond how it seems to him, if I can see its personal meaning for him, if I can sense the emotional flavor which it has for him . . . that is listening with understanding."

Carl Rogers

"Trust is people's ability to take risks in front of each other."

Chris Argyris

"Communications is not a thing . . . it is a process . . . the process of creating a meaning."

Dean Barnlund

Communications is such an all pervasive and dynamic ingredient of all human relations that it is difficult to consider it as a subject apart. In this book it has been intricately woven into the content of every chapter:

—*The Role of a Manager* is basically one of communication—the giving and receiving of information and sharing of experiences and meaning as they affect all else we do. The style of leadership determines the mode of communication.

—*The Organizational Climate* is determined by communications as they exist between manager and staff; staff and volunteers; staff and client; volunteer and client; and, volunteer and volunteer.

—*Motivation* is impossible to determine or maintain if a person is not effectively heard and the message acted upon; and

—*Planning, Evaluating, Job Design, Interviewing,* and *Training,* all are inextricably linked to effective communications.

Therefore, let us recognize that communications is not a new topic, but one which we shall simply consider from still more perspectives.

First, may I urge that we view communications as a friend, not an enemy. So much has been written about it and so many studies conducted pointing out the dangers and results of poor communication that it is easy to become a bit paranoid. One almost feels it is better to say nothing than to say the wrong thing, or to say the right thing the wrong way. But words—communication's tools—are one of the best ways we have of getting to know one another and of sharing our ideas and experiences and that's too precious a goal to abandon because of fear of inadequacy.

It is not that we negate the danger of poor communications. I thoroughly agree with Alfred Fleishman when he observed, "Because you have lived your entire life in a world of words, perhaps you think that you have no need to study their effect on you and

162

your nervous system. And yet people are destroyed physically and mentally by words every day, people who could have avoided many of their problems if they had understood more about what words do to them . . . words are the most important tool man has."[1]

That's just the point, if we can begin to understand and effectively deal with the tremendous impact our communications have on one another, then we can turn those negative effects around. Instead of destroying or diminishing people with words (or lack of them), we can build and free people with them and that is what good management is all about.

First, let us attempt to define what we mean by communications. It is perhaps most frequently thought of as simply transmitting a message (ideas, thoughts, attitudes, information, etc.) from one person to another. This sort of "message centered" communications implies that if the sender has a mastery and understanding of what facts and information he wishes to transmit, and is skillful and articulate in how this is done, success is almost assured. The emphasis is placed on the sender (or message formulator) instead of the receiver. Unfortunately a great many communicators operate out of this understanding.

However, many of the behavioral scientists and communications researchers have pointed out that the process is a bit more complex. They suggest the transactional approach which places the emphasis on the *meaning* being transmitted, rather than just on the message itself. The receiver is equally as important as the sender if this transaction is to occur.

Dean Barlund states that interpersonal communications is a process of meaning creating rather than idea or message sending. It occurs by "becoming personally involved, staying in as close and constant perceptual contact with the other persons present as you can, and trying to create conditions that will help the other people evoke meanings consonant with your intent and your perception of yourself, of others and of the situation."[2] It is therefore both interactive and dynamic—a people process, as opposed to a language process.

Peter Drucker states that communication entails four fundamentals:[3]

1. It is perception;
2. It is expectation;
3. It makes demands; and,

4. It is different than information, and largely opposite, yet interdependent.

Let us examine each briefly:

1. *Communication is perception.* This simply means it is the recipient, not the one who emits communication who communicates. Unless someone hears (that is *receives*) there is no communication, only noise. Our job in speaking and writing is to make it possible for the hearer or reader to perceive what we're saying. That means being clear—but more importantly, *relating the communication to the person's own experience, so he can perceive our meaning.* We have a terrible tendency to prepare our speeches, memos and reports in a vacuum, hardly considering who is to receive them, only what it is we want to say.

2. *Communication is expectation.* The human mind attempts to fit impressions and stimuli into a frame of expectations and resist the unexpected. We, therefore, must know what the recipient of our communication expects to see and hear so we can work within that framework. This is why participation in goal setting and planning of programs and evaluations of training are so valuable. It keeps us in the ballpark of expectations. *So we must listen first.*

3. *Communications makes demands.* The person initiating communication is always trying to get something across—an idea, attitude, program or action. The communication, then, always makes demands on the receiver, to become somebody, believe something, do something. So if the communication fits in with the aspirations, values and purposes of the receiver —it is powerful. If it does not, it is rejected.

4. *Communication and information are different and indeed largely opposite—yet interdependent.* Communication is perception, while information is logic (as well as impersonal and specific). Communication on the other hand, improves with the more levels of meaning it has. It may not be dependent on information at all (although it may) but may be purely shared experiences without any logic at all. *Perception rather than information is the prime factor in communication.*

Drucker sums up by stating that when and if our communications are firmly focused on the aspirations, values and motivation of those we communicate with, then it becomes effective. "Communication works only from one member of "us" to another, not from me to you."[4]

A Word About Words

It is not uncommon for a person to assume that the way to improve communications skills is to increase vocabulary. Since words are the tools of communication, adding more words should help. This overlooks the important reality that words in and by themselves cannot have meaning. Meaning resides in the minds of the people sending and receiving the words. Of the 600,000 words in the English language, 2,000 are used daily by an educated adult. The 500 most frequently used have 14,000 dictionary definitions.[5]

This illustrates one of the most frequent problems in communicating—instead of saying what does *it* (the word) mean, we should say what do *you* (the person) mean? For example—

"Too much government is bad for business." (How much is too much; which government; and, what business?)

or

"Volunteers take away paid jobs." (what volunteers; which jobs; how and when?)

In the book *Communications: The Transfer of Meaning*, Don Fabun points out two common causes of communication failure:[6]

1. *Assuming* that everyone knows what you are talking about; and,
2. *Assuming* you know what others are talking about (without asking questions to make sure).

Both of these overlook the crucial fact that individual experiences are never identical. So we see and hear things differently.

You've probably seen the poster that illustrates this point so well:

"I know you believe you understood what I think I said, but I am not sure you realize that what you heard is not what I meant."

Fabun suggests the following formulae to help alleviate distortion and misunderstanding. We must ask:

Who said so?

What did he say?

165

What did he mean?

How does he know?

Two critically important factors relating to the communication process are:

—*Interpersonal communications are inevitable* when two people are together. In other words it is impossible not to communicate. Even if you do not talk or look at the other person, you are communicating a very real message.

—*Interpersonal communications include both content and information about the content.* Tone of voice and body language speak very loudly about what is really meant by what is being said. If these are inconsistent with the words, then the message is apt to be scrambled.

If, for example, we congratulate a volunteer or staff member on a job well done and look preoccupied or move nervously on as quickly as possible, the result is a dual message—"I'm pleased—but not really".

It is so easy to forget that we communicate in several ways:

1. *By actual physical touch*—a tap on the shoulder, pat on the back, handshake, slap, spank, hug, etc.
2. *By visible movements of some part of our bodies*— (non-verbal —or body language)—point finger, wink, shrug, smile, hunch shoulders, scowl, fold arms, etc.
3. *By symbols which stand for something*—audible symbols, like speaking, crying, laughing or visible symbols such as the written word, pictures, graphs.

In other words, *everything* we do which transmits ideas or intentions to someone else is communications. As we said earlier, we cannot *not* communicate, the only question is what and how well.

John Powell, in his popular book *Why Am I Afraid To Tell You Who I Am?* identifies five levels of communications:[7]

Level Five—Cliché Conversation

This is the lowest level, with almost no authentic communication as there is almost no sharing of persons. It's the "Hi, how are you?", "How's it going?" "Let's get together soon" type so prevalent in our society of strangers. It's "people talking without speaking, people hearing without listening".

166

Level Four—Reporting the Facts About Others
Telling others what so and so has done or said with no personal comments of my own.

Level Three—My Ideas and Judgments
Carefully sharing some of myself, but being sure the decisions, opinions and ideas I offer are accepted. Playing it safe.

Level Two—Feelings and Emotions
("Gut Level"). Revealing the *feelings* that lie under my ideas and convictions which are uniquely my own. Telling who I really am.

Level One—Peak Communications
Absolute openness and honesty—"like two musical instruments playing exactly the same note, filled with and giving forth precisely the same sound".

But how do we move from inadequate functioning on Levels Three, Four and Five to the much more meaningful and fruitful first two levels?

Carl Rogers, the renowned counselor and writer, identifies three essential ingredients for this kind of communication:[8]

1. *Congruence.* This means you are what you are without masks, fronts or facade. Martin Buber identifies this as the difference between "being" and "seeming." He states, "to yield to seeming is man's essential cowardice; to resist it is his essential courage".[9]

   [Or, as a sage once said, "Be yourself—no one else is better qualified!"]

2. *Empathy.* This is the accurate, empathetic understanding of the other person. We must let the other person know we are interested and open not only to what they're saying, but also what they're feeling. But Rogers warns that this is risky, for if we really take this person's world into our own, we stand the chance of being changed ourselves, so we resist it.

3. *Positive Regard.* Having a warm, positive, accepting attitude toward the other person *as a person.* (Simply non-possessive caring.)

So it seems we must have a healthy knowledge, acceptance and affection for ourselves so that we might open up with understanding, acceptance and real interest to others.

I have found this to be true in both personal and group communications. The opening up of my "I" enables contact with your real "You" so that we become "Us."

In the book *Everybody Wins: Transactional Analysis Applied to Organizations*, there is the following free verse by Lyman K. Randall that clearly illustrates the problem:

Of Course I Believe

Trust you?
Sure I trust you!
(I wonder what he's after now.)

Be open with you?
Of course, I'm open with you!
(As open as I can be with a guy like you.)

Level with you?
You know I level with you!
(I'd like to more, but you can't take it.)

Accept you?
Naturally I accept you—just like you accept me.
(And when you learn to accept me, I might accept you more.)

Self-direction?
I've always believed in self-direction!
And some day this company may let us use some.

What's the hang-up?
Not a damn thing!
What could ever hang-up
   Two self-directing,
   Open, trusting,
   Leveling and accepting
     Guys like us?

Through open, honest communication we affirm ourselves as unique and valuable human beings and our uniqueness is clarified and affirmed.

Of course, there are risks involved in this. Not everyone is ready, or at a place personally, where they can deal effectively with this

168

type of communication. I think it is only realistic to expect that even though we might learn to be the kind of senders or initiators of Level One and Two communications described by Powell, the receivers may not be at that point yet and respond less than enthusiastically. If we anticipate and understand this when it occurs, perhaps we won't feel threatened or hurt or conclude that open communications is just another gimmick that doesn't work.

An example might be in giving negative feedback to a superior. This is extremely difficult and we avoid it whenever possible by convincing ourselves he or she really doesn't want to hear unpleasant things, especially about themselves or their actions. This might be absolutely right, but we must not make that assumption without checking it out. I have known high level people who long for honest feedback and almost never get it. One of the people I have valued most during my years as Director of our Center is a volunteer who serves as my truth teller or devil's advocate. When I ask for her response to an idea or project, I know it will be an honest one and that has had a significant effect on decisions involved. I encourage this feedback from both staff and volunteers and I, in turn, try to give them the same compliment. I trust them to be able to handle negative, as well as positive feedback and they do. (We call the negatives "opportunities for growth".) It doesn't always feel good, but we all need it and should value those who trust us enough to level with us.

Perhaps it is possible to accept this concept of open communication in personal, one-to-one encounters, but how about meetings and presentations in a group setting? Does "being" instead of "seeming" have anything to offer there? I feel strongly that it does. Based on years of sitting in twenty to thirty meetings per month, I can affirm that it is not until this open and trusting flow of information, ideas and feelings begins to occur that much of anything of significance happens. Games, turf battles, holding patterns, are rampant in community action and human service endeavors, just as they are in industry. We must face them as persons and agencies and refuse to endorse or participate in them. It is astounding what can happen when we do.

May I illustrate with an example from our community. Approximately three years ago the Director of Boulder Senior Citizens' Center and myself were asked by a national agency to convene a group of agencies serving senior citizens in our community. We were to consider how adequate services to seniors were and how they might

169

be expanded or improved so as to keep older persons in their own homes as opposed to institutionalizing them.

This particular group of agencies had traditionally communicated very sparingly, if at all, so the task was a challenging one. We kept the group very unstructured (no officers, by-laws, etc.) and simply requested that all participants be someone who could speak authoritatively for their agency. We then all agreed to: 1) share whatever information was needed by the group to assess our agency's service to seniors; 2) objectively evaluate the services as a whole and specifically in about two dozen categories (housing, health care, transportation, etc.); 3) based on this evaluation identify priorities for services to elderly in our community. This was all accomplished in about 6-9 months. We then decided as a group to try to implement or improve programs in all of the priority areas that we possibly could and formed interagency sub-committees to tackle them one at a time.

After three years, several innovative cooperative services have been launched (free adult health conferences, telephone reassurance, an inter-agency transportation council, nursing home task force, etc.). The astounding thing, however, is the level of trust in the group. Recently, five of these agencies read funding proposals in front of the entire group to receive input and endorsement before submitting for state and federal funding. Even more encouraging is the fact that the input was accepted and acted upon, even though it meant scrapping one of the proposals altogether. The commitment has remained very high on the part of group members and several agency directors have stated it is one of the most productive and rewarding group endeavors they have participated in for years.

And I feel as strongly about the relevance of this authentic approach of honest communication applied to speeches and presentations. I'm not suggesting we use these as opportunities to unload all our own feelings, emotions, hangups and causes on the audience. What I am saying is, each of us has a unique contribution to make because our own particular background brings certain insights and perspectives as we view any topic or subject we're asked to address. If we are only a conduit for the ideas of others, we rob our audiences. We again must share something of ourselves if it is to be meaningful and truly effective.

I have seen this work in some very difficult and even hostile group situations: when I addressed black ex-convicts; in a training session for state and regional officials who were resisting the training; with

170

an outspoken group of 350 in a largely rural state who were tired of being talked down to; and with reluctant funding agents. In all of these, and the other training and speeches I've given, I try to follow two cardinal rules: 1) know the material I'm being asked to speak about; and, 2) be myself as I present it. (At least then if they don't like me—it's really me and not someone I've tried to imitate.) Some of the questions I ask myself in preparing such a speech or presentation are:

1. Why am I the one who was asked to do this particular session? What are the expectations?

2. What information, knowledge or experience do I have that would be helpful for me to share, in line with their intent and expectations? Who needs to be involved in the planning?

3. How can I best insure that I'll have active listeners vs. passive hearers? What content, strategies, type and variety of sessions and preparation would insure that *the audience and I will both be enthusiastic about what is occuring?* How can I be sure that the "message does not go out from the notes of the speaker to the notes of the listener without going through the minds of either of us?"[11]

4. How can I make what I have to say as interesting and vital as possible? Include such things as:

   —Make concise and precise points. No verbal meandering. (There is an old saying among writers—if you have difficulty with a sentence it means your thinking is confused. It is not the sentence that needs straightening out, it is the thought behind it!)

   —Utilize clear progression of thought.

   —Use plain talk—not jargon.

   —Use pertinent and appropriate quotations to make more interesting.

   —Research topic for current, meaningful input.

   —Stick to time allotted and subject to be covered.

   —Use examples and illustrations from real life experiences (referred to as "war stories"). Bring from theoretical to practical.

   —Maintain eye contact so the "speech" can become a conversation geared to their needs and reactions.

171

5. How can "I be me" and yet recognize and respond to the individuality and personality of each different group?

Whether we consider one-to-one or group communications, there is no denying it is an extremely complex and fragile process which can break down at any number of points. Some of the more common barriers or blocks might be:

1. *Distance and/or inaccessibility.*

   If the Director of Volunteers or the supervisor of a department is either physically or psychologically separated from the staff and volunteers, there is little opportunity for essential face to face contact. Being unavailable when staff or volunteers need to talk is a sure way to endanger effective communications.

2. *Distortion.*

   This is the common difficulty of confusing facts and feelings. Are we reacting to what was said, or to what we thought was meant by what was said, due to filters, opinions, and prejudices?

3. *Lack of Trust and Leveling.*

   Failure to say what we really feel or what we know needs to be said due to fear of how it will be received. This is especially troublesome if we have to give the boss unpleasant news (upward communication). There is also a tendency to feel volunteers only want to hear when they have done well and are unable to receive constructive criticism. (Untrue!)

4. *Hidden Agendas.*

   When either the sender or receiver come with a hidden agenda, the communication is very apt to be superficial and manipulative. The outcome has been pre-determined in this person's mind and the conversation is simply to get others to concur with it.

5. *Ineffective Listening.*

   In a helpful publication *Troubled Talk* by Alfred Fleishman, the following poem illustrates the problem:[12]

   "The person who attends a concert with his mind on business hears, but does not really hear.

   "The person who walks amidst a song of birds and thinks only of what he will have for dinner hears, but doesn't really hear.

"The man who listens to the words of his friends or his wife or his child and doesn't catch the note of urgency—'notice me, help me, care about me'—hears, but doesn't really hear.

"The man who listens to the news and thinks only of how it will affect the stock market hears, but does not really hear."

Someone has suggested that the greatest frontier of communication is not in developing good talkers—but good listeners. One of the very real difficulties is that the average speaker speaks at a rate of 150-200 words per minute and the average listener can receive 1,000 words per minute. Because of this tremendous gap, most people develop some very bad listening habits (many of which are listed in Chapter VII).

6. *Believing Something Must Be So Just Because We (or Someone Else) Say It Is*—without asking questions, exploring alternatives, examining the source.

7. *Using the "Allness Syndrome".*
   Indicating that since we already know all about the subject, there's no need for further discussion. Or using generalizations to cover all specifics—"All volunteers are unreliable because they're unpaid"; "All staff resents volunteers"; or "If you've seen one—you've seen 'em all!"

8. *Either/Or Syndrome.*
   Believing there are only two sides to every question and neglecting to examine the in-betweens.

9. *Frozen Images.*
   Believing what was is!

10. *Gaps Between People.*
    Allowing differences between generations, cultures, or races, to hamper communications.

Although I have concentrated primarily on verbal communications in this Chapter, we must not overlook the vital importance of our written communications as well. Memos, reports, newsletters, notices, news articles, brochures and letters are a part of our everyday world of work and we must learn to do them well. Here is a place where help is usually readily available, if we ask for the right thing at the right place. I have found the following to be fruitful recruiting grounds:

—*Brochures, news articles or ads*—Approach advertising agencies and graphics departments of large industries. (Our Center has been the non-paying client of an ad agency for a year and has also gotten all of our graphics done free by an expert from a local company.)

—*Newsletters, articles*—Contact university or college journalism classes or advertise for volunteers with journalism training. Put an ad in "Help Wanted" and state the qualifications clearly— also identify that it is volunteer.

—*Reports, Grants, Annual Reports*—Seek advice and assistance from the business leaders or professionals on your Board. They can be especially helpful when preparing reports, graphs, and charts, to be used in funding requests. They know what they would need and want to know if they were the person receiving it.

Generally speaking, the most common problem in written communications is a failure to be *concise* and *clear*. Verbosity clouds the essential "who, what, when, where and how" that we need to convey. Self-discipline is a must and sometimes this can best be achieved by jotting down a simple outline before drafting the report, letter or article.

Some helpful questions might be: What are the essential points to cover? What is the most logical sequence to present them in? Have I been as concise as possible? Is the format and wording as interesting as possible? Will the person receiving it get the message *and* the meaning?

One of the cardinal rules I have used in written communications is that everything leaving our office must be as attractive, neat and accurate as possible. People judge an office and the staff by what it receives from you. Sloppy, poorly worded, careless communications create an image that is difficult, if not impossible, to erase. Likewise good communications have an extremely positive impact.

One theory of interpersonal relations and communications which looks at and attempts to understand the things people do and say to each other is transactional analysis (TA). It has been utilized by therapists for some time and more recently by trainers in industries such as Association Merchandising Corp., American Airlines and The Bank of New York.[13]

The fundamental theory is that each person (or personality) is constituted of three *ego states*. An ego state is defined as a consistent pattern of behavior based upon prior feelings and experiences.

174

Whatever ego state is in control at any given time determines a person's reaction to a particular situation. These three ego states are: the Parent, the Adult and the Child.

The Parent is learned from a person's parents and other people who are important during childhood in guiding our early experiences. The Parent is an authority figure and might be rebuking, nurturing, punitive, or consoling. "This ego state is one of superiority, authority and command. The Parent likes to be in control and to be right."[14]

The Child ego state grows out of one's own early childhood experiences. The Child represents an immature ego state and is one of irresponsibility and sometimes playfulness which might demonstrate itself in being rebellious, compliant, excited or enthusiastic.

The Adult ego state is the mature, objective, reality-based thinking state which helps us use past experience to make rational and appropriate responses to present situations.

TA helps analyze the transactions or interactions between people to see where and how communications become crossed or ineffective and then provides a base of understanding to help improve them. "It seeks to instill in people a facility in dealing with people on a straightforward, responsible, authentic basis."[15]

This concept is far too complex to deal with effectively here, but may I recommend some references that cover the subject in depth:

I'm OK—You're OK: A Practical Guide to Transactional Analysis, by Thomas A. Harris; *Born To Win,* by Muriel James and Dorothy Jongeward; and, *Everybody Wins: Transactional Analysis Applied To Organizations* by Dorothy Jongeward.

As we deal specifically with communications for the Director of Volunteers, we make two assumptions: (1) you have something to say; and, (2) there is someone to say it to. It would seem that if we spent more time determining the "what" of (1) and the "who" of (2), the problem of "how" to communicate would be much easier to solve.

In volunteer programs, there are at least five groups that we must be prepared to communicate with:

1. Volunteers
2. Paid staff
3. Agency administration
4. Clients
5. The community

Different things need to be communicated to each of these groups, because their needs and interests in the volunteer program differ a great deal. A mistake is made when we assume that communication means "laying a message on someone." That message must be received and understood or real communication has not taken place.

Let's look for a moment at *what* you might need to communicate with each of these groups, and then see if that suggests some methods that might be effective in accomplishing this.

WHO	WHAT	HOW
VOLUNTEERS	Information about agency needs and volunteer opportunities.	Group presentations or personal interview.
	Receive information regarding volunteer's skills and needs regarding placement and goal setting.	Personal interview.
	Orientation of volunteer regarding job, agency policies, and programs.	Written pamphlets, handbooks, and conversations with Volunteer Director, staff, and volunteer. Visual aides.
	Training.	Skills workshops, role play, lectures, visual aides, on-job training by staff and other volunteers.
	Evaluation.	Written (on form for personnel file) or verbal interviews—include supervisor of volunteer.
	Internal information.	Newsletter, house organ, bulletin boards, group meetings, "grapevine."
	Recognition.	Group recognition (i.e.. luncheons, picnics, parties, outings—administration should be present); individual certificates, notes, and conversations. Promotion is ultimate reward.
ADMINISTRATION and/or BOARD OF DIRECTORS	Value of the volunteer program to the agency (Need for administration's "blessing" is crucial.)	Succinct and well-planned verbal presentation. Use graphs and charts when possible to depict $ and manpower benefits.
	Needs of volunteer program regarding staff, funds, space etc.	Present clearly defined plan and why the funds, space and people are needed. Relate benefits to agency and clients.

176

WHO	WHAT	HOW
	Goals of volunteer program.	Written report regarding goals (short and long range). Tell who plans to do what and when.
	Statistics and expenditures.	Monthly written reports to administration and Board.
	Accomplishments of the volunteer program.	Copies of all P.R. of interest, i.e., news releases, human interest stories, newsletters. Include administration in recognition ceremonies.
PAID STAFF	Planning for volunteer program.	Staff or small group meetings. Individual interviews regard staff needs.
	Orientation/training regarding effective use of volunteers as staff.	Role play, small group meetings, visual aides (movies, slides, closed circuit TV), problem-solving sessions.
	Staff supervision of volunteers.	Periodic verbal or written follow-up with both staff and volunteers. Provide consultation as needed.
	Evaluation of volunteers.	Written forms or periodic interviews; report memos should be filed in volunteer's file.
CLIENT*	Planning for volunteer program.	Individual or small group meetings to explore clients' needs and attitudes regarding volunteers.
	Matching volunteer to client.	Interview with each individually, if possible, or with staff person working most closely with the client.
	Evaluation of volunteer placement.	Questionnaire (anonymous occasionally) or periodic conversations with client and/or staff.

*This is a key component in the communications network of volunteer programs that is frequently overlooked. If the volunteer is not enhancing or extending your agency's service to the client you are missing the mark!

WHO	WHAT	HOW
COMMUNITY	Information about your agency and its volunteer program.	Speeches to clubs, churches, schools, etc.; newspaper articles, radio interviews, and spot announcements; posters, pictorial displays, slides, movies, billboards, car stickers, flyers, and brochures.
	Invitation to support your program with manpower and $s.	Same as above, followed by phone or individual interviews with anyone indicating an interest. Fund solicitations by phone or mail (not "canned," hopefully).

As Directors of Volunteers, we have the responsibility to be the catalyst to see that open and healthy communications exist between all of these affected segments of the program. It is through our interactions with one another that a sense of mutual or shared purpose begins to emerge. We become a team in the finest sense because each person involved is committed to goals and programs they helped plan and are actively involved in carrying out and evaluating. This encourages a sense of ownership which enhances the chances of success in any program or endeavor. The PLAN-DO-EVALU-ATE process, when done in concert by all concerned, represents communications at its finest.

We must never overlook or underestimate the importance of what we are about. Volunteerism is one of the last vital strongholds of democracy in this country today. If we are ineffective or apologetic in articulating what we have and still can accomplish through the voluntary involvement of people who care—then we have ultimately failed those we lead.

References

1. Fleishman, Alfred, *Sense and Nonsense*, International Society for General Semantics, 1971.

2. Barnlund, Ean, quoted from an article in *Bridges Not Walls: A Book About Interpersonal Communication*, edited by John Stewart, Addison-Wesley, 1973, p. 16.

3. Drucker, Peter, *Management: Tasks, Responsibilities, Practices*, Harper & Row, 1973, p. 483 ff.

4. Ibid, p. 493.

5. Fabun, Don, *Communications: The Transfer of Meaning*, Glencoe Press, 1968, p. 27.

6. Ibid, p. 33.

7. Powell, John, *Why Am I Afraid To Tell You Who I Am?*, Argus Com-
   1969, p. 50-85.

8. *Bridges Not Walls*, p. 255.

9. Ibid, p. 285.

10. Ibid, p. 82.

11. Odiorne, George, Tape series, *What Every Manager Should Know*,
    "Communications", MBO, Inc. 1973.

12. Fleishman, Alfred, *Troubled Talk*, International Society for General
    Semantics, 1973, p. 7.

13. Rush, Harold and McGroth, Phyllis, *Transactional Analysis Moves Into
    Corporation Training*, an article in The 1973 Conference Board Record,
    p. 38 ff.

14. Ibid.

15. Ibid.

CHAPTER X

Putting It All Together: Client/Staff/Volunteer/Board

Have you ever attended a concert, play or ballgame which was so well done that you went away feeling you had experienced something exceptional? Usually when this occurs it is that the unique and separate talents of all those involved were somehow blended into a whole that was greater than all of its parts. Each musician, actor or ball player was important, knew his or her part, and performed with excellence and spirit—but acknowledged their interrelatedness with one another. How rare and beautiful that is!

It is exactly such a goal I would set for human service organizations and the volunteer programs within them—to be highly skilled and creative teams . . . the effective instruments for meeting human need in our communities.

It would be nice, although somewhat cowardly, for me to end the book on that lofty note, leaving the reader to struggle alone with how this might be achieved. I realize all too well what a difficult goal that is and, although I have no pat answers or magic solutions, we can attempt some serious thinking on the subject together.

Perhaps the most sensible starting place is to be sure we know who all of the players are. By examining them separately first, perhaps we will have more success when we attempt to "blend their separate talents into a whole greater than its parts." These are: the client; the staff; the volunteers; and, the Board of Directors. (There may be others in some instances, but at least these are the principal ones we will deal with here.)

The Client

I begin here because the client (or consumer—receiver of services) is the *reason for the organization's being,* and yet he/she is the most universally overlooked of all. At some point in time, the needs of the group of people you serve (juvenile delinquents, educationally handicapped, disaster victims, mentally ill, elderly, battered children, etc.) became so important to some group in your community that an agency or service was established especially designed to meet that need. The people involved in setting up the service were clearly committed to this particular cause and fought to do something about it. Frequently these were families of persons with the need, volunteers who identified with it and agencies with related concerns.

However, as these services grow, hierarchies begin to form and clients find themselves further and further removed from the people who make decisions about the services designed for them. (A hierarchy has been described as "a system where information goes up through a series of filters, and commands and prohibitions come down through a series of loudspeakers."[1]) Unfortunately, planning "for" instead of "with" clients is not the exception but the rule in agencies today.

The trend must be reversed if human services are not to fail altogether. Too frequently grants are written and programs added because the agency needs the funding or legislation dictates it, and not because the client legitimately needs (or wants) the service purchased by those funds. There is too much real need going unmet to engage in this practice any longer.

The place to start is with the funding agencies—whether they be United Funds, foundations or governmental bodies. *Needs must be assessed before funding is allotted* so that the limited dollars we do have for human services can go to meet real needs. The people who need to be intimately involved in this process of assessment are

182

clients themselves. No amount of "study about" or "researching of" can acquaint a person with a need as can living with it.

Clients must also be included in the volunteer programs in our agencies. They must have input into the planning of the program, so client needs will be met and services extended and enriched by the volunteer involvement. The way to determine if this is in fact happening is to also involve the client in evaluating the program at strategic intervals.

Some of the more adventuresome agencies are also discovering the client has another important contribution to make, as a giver as well as receiver of service. Client-volunteers are now proving extremely successful in mental health settings, welfare programs, day care centers, Headstart programs, juvenile offender programs, etc. The empathy, sensitivity and caring these people bring to others is tremendous and the self-esteem it generates in them is vital to their becoming full partners in society. *We must seek to extend the opportunity of giving to everyone.* But to do this, we need to be realistic regarding providing necessary out-of-pocket expenses or exploring appropriate stipended volunteer programs (i.e., Retired Senior Volunteer Program, Foster Grandparents, Vista) that make it financially feasible for non-traditional volunteers to do so.

The Staff

A. *Director of Volunteers.* The bulk of material presented thus far has been designed to establish the fact that this person is, in fact, a manager of human resources and as such needs to develop the skills and knowledge to be an effective manager.

Acknowledging the unfortunate reality that in many agencies this position is filled haphazardly, regarded lightly and provided little staff and administrative support or training, I still maintain that *it is one of the most important and potentially influential positions in human services today.*

Like it or not, the future of volunteerism is in our hands. This is an awesome responsibility, if you agree with Eduard Lindeman when he said, "I wish I knew how to induce volunteers to appreciate the significant role they play in furnishing vitality to the democratic enterprise. They are to Democracy what circulation of the blood is to the organism. *They keep Democracy alive.*"[2]

Are we up to preserving and nourishing this vital life blood of democracy in a society changing as radically and rapidly as ours? In my opinion it will take a dedication and determination reminiscent of the early days of this country. We, and the volunteers we lead, must once again become pace setters, bringing fresh ideas and vigor to weary communities and organizations.

Some critical questions those of us in the field of volunteer administration need to examine are:

—Are we ready to acknowledge that we are, in fact, managers of precious human resources and committed to improving the skills required to be effective?

—Are we concerned about enabling all who work with us to develop their fullest potentialities through

* designing meaningful and needed jobs for them to do (being sensitive to their needs for achievement, recognition, accomplishment and challenging work);
* providing training and growth opportunities;
* supervising in a fair and sensitive fashion;
* delegating creatively and well;
* involving everyone in decisions affecting them; and
* encouraging open and honest communication?

—Will we accept the responsibility of being those essential "linking pins"—bringing staff, volunteers, client and community into meaningful dialogue and cooperation?

—Will we strive to be innovators—the "doers and movers" instead of simply program conduits or imitators? This field is at that dynamic point of growth and change where it cries for those leaders whom Greenleaf describes as "better than most at pointing the direction."

—Can we see beyond the present realities of program to envision future implications and outcomes, "looking up from work and outward toward goals?"

I am convinced, based on hundreds of conversations with Directors of volunteer programs the past seven years, that most of us will confront the issues squarely and tackle them eagerly. But the size of the task before us demands our best efforts, not only individually, but as a group. We therefore must extend present channels of interchange of ideas, knowledge and support and develop new ones. We need each other as never before!

B. *Other Paid Staff.* The place to begin in assessing the impact of paid staff on a volunteer program is at the very top—Administration. Attitudes of top administrators vary regarding volunteers all the way from open hositility to vague lip service to avid commitment. This attitude is generally subtly reflected throughout the organization and is therefore of utmost importance to the volunteer program. Sometimes Administrators are reluctant about volunteer participation because of lack of information and involvement. They should be the first ones consulted about adding or expanding such a program and then kept appropriately and imaginatively informed of all progress, accomplishments, and yes, even problems. After all, they are responsible for the organization and therefore have a need (and a right) to know about anything that affects it.

May I suggest that there are ways to move a reluctant Administrator from vague acceptance, or even opposition, to a greater understanding and commitment. You might invite them to a good meeting or workshop on Volunteer Management sponsored by a local college, Volunteer Coordinators' Association or Voluntary Action Center. Be sure they get copies of all press releases relating to your volunteer program. Plan to have them meet and talk with some of your best volunteers in informal idea exchange sessions and attend occasional Advisory Committee Meetings. Present all requests and reports in a businesslike and professional fashion. Ask for what you need in a clear and decisive fashion and reciprocate by reporting in a meaningful way the return on the investment to the agency.

The rest of paid staff is also critically important to the volunteer program, for without their acceptance and cooperation, it cannot possibly succeed. Volunteers do not function in a vacuum and are vitally affected by the climate of the organization, reflecting the atttiudes of staff toward them.

The key is *cooperation and coordination* instead of *competition.* As we have indicated throughout the book, this is accomplished by encouraging staff involvement in:

—*planning* the volunteer program;

—*training* (participating in training sessions for volunteers and for staff on the use of volunteers);

—*supervising* volunteers assigned to them in a conscientious and creative fashion;

—*communicating* with the volunteers and Office of Volunteers regarding progress and problems, and

—*evaluating* the volunteer program.

Generally, if staff members can simply accept the fact that volunteers are persons with the same needs, motives, and capabilities as anyone else (as opposed to considering them "those nice free people") then acceptance as co-workers will be much easier. *Standards must not be lowered for volunteers,* for we usually get what we expect. Volunteers are not there to replace staff, but to enrich and extend it. Their investment of time and ability makes it possible for paid staff to have more time to do the things they do best. That's creative partnership.

The Volunteers

Harriet Naylor makes this cogent observation: "Volunteering *can* be an exciting, growing, enjoyable experience. It is truly gratifying to serve a cause, practice one's ideals, work with people of like interests to solve problems together, see benefits and know one had a hand in them. . . . People do things they didn't dream they could do; they feel a stake in community achievement. Never underestimate the power of a volunteer who is well placed, and trained for the job!"[3]

Throughout this book I have tried to advocate for the rights of the volunteer:

* the right of being offered the opportunity to become a volunteer regardless of race, financial status, sex or age;
* the right to be carefully interviewed and appropriately assigned to a meaningful job;
* the right to expect training and supervision to enable them to perform the job well;
* the right to be involved in planning and evaluating the
* program they participate in;

* the right to receive recognition in a way that is meaningful to them; and

* the right to be regarded as persons, with individuality, uniqueness and value.

Perhaps it is now appropriate to deal with the equally important aspect of volunteering—responsibility. As we all know, rights bring with them responsibility. It is essential that the volunteer fulfill his or her part of this bargain of creative partnership with staff with integrity and diligence if it is to work successfully.

In order to do that, may I suggest the following to the volunteer:

—Be honest and open with the Director of Volunteers and other staff, beginning with the interview, regarding intent, goals, needs and skills so that a good placement is possible;

—Understand the requirements of time and duties of assignments *before* accepting them and once accepting, fulfill the commitment to the best of your ability;

—Work to deserve being treated as a recognized and respected member of the team (no room for temperamental prima donnas, off-and-on again types or "no shows");

—Take the commitment seriously enough to participate in planning and evaluating the volunteer program and in whatever training or learning opportunities are available;

—Share ideas with staff, for the volunteer frequently has a fresh, new perspective that is valuable. However, do not be hurt or resentful if the ideas are not always implemented, for staff's ideas aren't always either;

—View staff as allies and mentors for much can be learned from them;

—Respect the confidentiality of the agency and its clients;

—Seek and accept honest feedback on performance. Remember, negative feedback is valuable too, when viewed as opportunities for growth;

—Serve as goodwill ambassadors and interpreters for the agency and its services in the community-at-large;

—Be informed and therefore more effective advocates of change when change is needed; and,

—Bring "the priceless gift of service and enthusiasm which lightens the load for all."[4]

The Board of Directors

This is probably the segment of the organization that is most difficult to define and deal with, even though it is of utmost importance. It is basically a group of people (most frequently volunteers) who serve as the policy making body of the organization. In many instances it is legally responsible for the actions and operation of the agency. The reason it is difficult to present anything very definitive on this subject is that the status, structure, and role of boards are in a state of turmoil at this point.

This is not new, however, for boards of human service organizations have proceeded through various evolutions in the past:[5]

—originally they were composed of doers and financial contributors;

—then financial contributors only, who had no program responsibility (prestigious boards);

—during the Depression the move was toward 'working' boards;

—later returned to contributors and the 'names' in the community;

—as government funding, United Funds and grants increased, members no longer needed to financially support the agency and became a sort of honorary group with no clearly definable function; often rubber stamps for staff decisions; and

—now trend seems to be reversing again, to broader citizen and client participation and working, functioning boards.

Board membership, structure and functions vary depending on whether the agency or organization is an industry, a privately owned organization (called the private sector), government agency, or not-for-profit organization. An excellent resource book, recently published, which deals with Boards of Directors of both industry and public agencies is *The Effective Director in Action*.[6] It spells out the dilemmas, rights, responsibilities and challenges of boards in a clear and most provocative fashion.

This issue of Boards of Directors needs to be dealt with seriously, for they are under fire in both the business and voluntary sectors. According to Peter Drucker, the one thing most boards have in common today is that *they do not function*. "The decline of the board

188

is a universal phenomenon of this century."[7] He states that nothing shows this more clearly than the fact that in many of the great business catastrophies in this century, the boards (although the legal governing organ of a corporation) were the last to know. This happened with Austria's leading bank, Rolls-Royce of England, Penn-Central in the United States and with Italy's leading chemical company. He goes on, "the board, whatever its name, and whatever its legal structure, has become a fiction."[8]

These are extremely harsh indictments and although he was speaking primarily of boards in industry, those of us in human services must heed the warning. I have been astounded in workshops all over the country, and also in various surveys of needs of Directors of volunteer programs, that board/staff relationships is the number one concern again and again. And the issue is raised by volunteers and staff alike.

One of the primary difficulties seems to be one of interrelationships that are unclear and often misunderstood. The staff is not sure which decisions it is to make and carry out and which should be reserved for board action. The board generally suffers from vague and ill-defined parameters of its jurisdiction and responsibility. So mistrust is fostered. Situations develop such as an executive who usurps board prerogatives; a board which threatens and intimates an insecure administrator; or prestigious boards whose members are there for the honor, while the harried staff longs for a working board.

One of the strains on the executives today is the maze of reporting responsibilities he or she has to contend with:[9]

—the Board of Directors;
—the boards and executives of all agencies supplying funds to their agency;
—officials and political appointees (if it is a government agency or receives funding from these people);
—local officials and legislators;
—the average citizen—the community at large.

The sheer logistics of trying to cope with this maze can be overwhelming and tempt the most conscientious executive to short circuit communications channels whenever possible.

189

The prime ingredients in a good board/staff relationship would seem to be:

* Clearly defined and agreed upon role expectations for both;

* A strong sense of trust and respect for the value of these roles;

* An understanding of being mutually responsible to each other; and,

* Open and honest communications.

In *The Effective Director in Action,* Zusman suggests that the day of the "honorary board" which met a few times a year to participate occasionally in fund-raising events or act as spokesman for an agency program is gone forever. He states that the makeup of public agency boards has become a central issue in establishing and setting directions for new agencies and he predicts (and we are already witnessing) that board membership of a modern agency will soon represent a cross section of the social makeup of the community. "Board membership no longer is just an honorary and ceremonial position. It is a complex, difficult, time-consuming, often frustrating task, with great responsibility and little recompense other than the satisfaction of involvement . . . it still remains an honor, but now it has become an opportunity that can be openly sought and fought for."[10]

What are some of the functions that boards should legitimately assume? Although there are obviously numerous variables, depending on the situation, these are generally agreed upon by the few writers who address the subject:[11]

1. *Carry out the functions and obligations as designated by law or charter.*

   Zusman points out that public agency boards rarely have clear legal status. To determine a board's status, government agencies must search the laws and regulations which established the agency. In voluntary agencies, the duties and responsibilities of the board are usually spelled out in the charter (but not always). He sees a current trend toward written descriptions of board roles and for legal specifications of authority for agency boards.

190

2. *Serve as a review body to counsel, advise and deliberate with top management (administration) regarding agency policy and operations.*

    It needs to take the pulse of the organization, to watch its spirit and be sure it is progressing toward agreed upon goals.

3. *Set policy, authorize operational goals and objectives, and emphasize quality of overall corporate planning in the organization.*

4. *Encourage the executive to establish rules and procedures* for the administration of the agency and see that they are followed.

5. *Serve as a public and community relations organization.*

    This means members need to have access to (or in some cases be a member of) the constituents and publics of the organization—to hear from them and talk to them. This is necessary both to be able to interpret the organization to the public and the concerns and needs of the constituents to the organization. The organization must not operate in a vacuum.

6. *Monitor operations of the agency.*

    This includes having access to necessary information regarding budget, program, problems and achievements so it can objectively evaluate the executive and the agency itself. The members need to be prepared to ask penetrating questions.

7. *Support the agency in the growing competition for funds.*

    Appropriate board representatives should accompany and support the executive in funding hearings. In certain instances they may want to make the presentation.

8. *Act as "ambassadors, negotiators, and intermediaries between the agency and elements in the community whenever problems arise."*[12]

    At times, this may mean taking a stand against some action that the agency is being pressured to carry out even though it is against agency policy (especially when this requires fighting a battle with politically influential people).

9. *In some agencies the board has primary responsibility for finances.*

   The treasurer must keep financial records; prepare financial statements and reports; prepare budgets (together with staff); and safeguard the agency's financial assets through bonding, insurance and internal controls.

Another helpful reference in examining the whole gamut of board functions and responsibilities is *The Board Member— Decision Maker for the Non-Profit Organization.*[13]

It is important to acknowledge here that many volunteer programs are a part of larger organizations which have Boards of Directors. It is extremely valuable for the volunteer program to have its own Advisory Committee which, although it has no legal responsibilities, can offer tremendous assistance to the Director of Volunteers, in planning, evaluating and implementing the program. Membership should include clients, volunteers and staff.

The important thing to remember is that there must be clearly defined and viable channels of communications from this Advisory group to the Board of Directors (such as the Chairman becoming an automatic member of the Board, etc.). If this is not done, your Advisory group and volunteer program will not have direct input into decision making mechanisms and therefore be unable to impact decisions that vitally affect you.

Harriet Naylor offers this positive statement of possibilities for boards and executives:

   "A well chosen and well trained Board confidently expects stimulating leadership from qualified professionals. From give-and-take during informal discussions, both develop trust in the ultimate decisions. Able professionals are encouraged to experiment with pioneer programs when they know their Boards will be secure enough to be interested in learning from failure as well as hearing about success. Each enables the other at the administrative level."[14]

Or as Robert Greenleaf says, if a strong board sets distinction of the institution as the goal, invests the time and energy, organizes itself for the task and stays with it, distinction is practically assured.[15]

192

Putting It All Together.

We have thus far attempted to define the various essential elements of this intricate organism called a human service agency (and most especially its volunteer program). When the responsibilities, rights and difficulties of each segment are examined, the problem of blending them all together into a smoothly functioning, harmonious whole becomes apparent—*and yet it must be done.*

As we said in the beginning of this Chapter, the key would seem to be for each person in the organization to "know their part and play it with excellence and spirit," so that the blend of talents might enrich and enable the whole. *There is no one right plot or design for an organization or a volunteer program.* Each must be flexible enough to respond to their own realities of persons, funding, community needs and vision. What we are talking about is 'synergy'— the ability of a group to out-perform even its own best individual resource. *The one absolutely essential element would seem to be trust!* "Nothing will move until trust is firm."[16]

Since this sounds so logical and sensible, why is it so difficult to achieve? It has astounded me time and again to hear members of the same organization (Board Chairman and Executive; staff and volunteers; client and staff) relate to each other as "the enemy" . . . the one to out-maneuver.

I personally feel many of these frictions stem from people's basic distrust of one another and some firmly engrained Theory "X" assumptions about people. Without trust, we box one another in. We diminish others and ourselves, when relationships are dictated and defined by sacred rule books and organization charts. When we forget to relate to one another as *people first* and as staff, client, volunteer or board member secondly, then roles get in the way of trust and synergism. To blend, we must give up some of ourselves and receive some of others. Rigidity, suspicion or jealousy make this blending impossible to achieve, for "I" become so intent on validating "me" that I cannot relate to "us".

The critical truth that seems so elusive is this—when one member grows and develops, we all grow or when one member is diminished, we all are. It is trust that is the cornerstone of synergistic harmony.

Are there any thoughts we might share for bringing about the goal of an integrated, fully functioning team? I think there are.

As Koontz and O'Donnell point out "the actions of groups are, in reality the actions of men [and women] who manage them, and these actions emanate from the principles and convictions of those who exercise power within them . . . there is no action without personal action."[17] In other words, it starts with each one of us personally.

There is no denying that change is often painful, but it is just as often exhilarating. And it does not just happen, it has to be caused. Antony Jay, in his book *Management and Machiavelli* observes that there are two kinds of change—imitative or creative (following or leading). And he goes on to say change is not a sideline of leadership, it is an integral part of it. "Leading the whole organization needs wisdom and flair and vision that cannot be reduced to a system and incorporated into a training manual."[18]

One strategy gaining in use is the task force (or task group) approach. This is combining people from different departments and different levels of the organization into a semi-autonomous group that is usually temporary. These groups differ from traditional committees in several ways. They are more task oriented, they cut across organization lines, and they generally have some responsibility and authority to help implement the decisions they generate.

In an article entitled "The Many Uses of Task Forces", Thomas L. Quick states, "Probably no other organizational form offers as much to the executive seeking more effective solutions to problems, more profitable decisions, more ways to explore and exploit opportunities, as the task force."[19]

Some of the benefits that accrue to the organization through this approach are developing and training potential managers and volunteer leaders; enriching and enlarging the jobs of those taking part (both paid staff and volunteer); evaluating the performance and potential of the members; and, more fully utilizing all the skills of people who may otherwise be under-utilized.

As I have mentioned throughout the book, we utilize the task force approach extensively at our Volunteer and Information Center and attribute to it much of our growth, flexibility and vitality as an agency. We combine this strategy in our Advisory Committee structure. Once a task has been identified that needs special attention (i.e., recruitment of teen volunteers, senior involvement, volunteers in elementary schools) the job is carefully defined and a person is sought out to lead that task force who has the skill, background, interest and time to commit to the job. As soon as they accept the task force leadership they become a member of the Advisory Committee. All appointments are made for one year, but the person can

194

be reappointed. Each year the Advisory Committee and staff re-evaluates all task forces to see which need to be dropped, extended or continued as is, or if new ones need to be added.

The Task Force Leader helps to identify appropriate people to work with him or her on the task. On our Youth Task Force, for example, we have members from staff, adults working with youth from the schools and community, and teenagers from the high schools. So there is Advisory Committee, staff, volunteer and client representation. Similarily in our Senior Involvement Task Force (now Retired Senior Volunteer Program) we have seniors, agency professionals serving the elderly, and staff.

The delightful thing I have experienced about this system is that it enables people involved to perform at an extremely high level of cooperation and commitment. It eliminates petty in-fighting because everyone knows their job and recognizes their dependency and inter-relatedness with others in the organization. It, in my opinion, represents voluntarism at its finest. It promotes success through diversity rather than conformity and enables the people involved to develop to their fullest potential.

It is also an excellent way to revitalize a "bored" board. Many times shifting from being a traditional prestigious board to a working board is difficult to achieve, even when this is desired. Through the task force approach, the opportunity can be extended to board members to become actively and vitally involved in program areas for a designated period of time and for a specific reason. They join staff members, clients and other appropriate people in addressing a particular problem or challenge. Interest and commitment generally soar as the involved board members get a clearer sense of their contribution, as well as a greater knowledge of the agency.

But I may sound a word of warning here. It is precisely at the point that we arrive at this ultimate goal of unanimity of purpose and coordinated efforts that we fall prey to another danger. This is what Irving Janis calls "group think". He says the more amiability and ésprit de corps there is among members of a policy-making in-group, the greater the danger that independent critical thinking will be replaced by group think (defined as "the desperate drive for concensus at any cost that suppresses dissent among the mighty in the corridors of power.")[20] Some danger signals according to Janis are:

—*Invulnerability*. The feeling the group cannot lose and therefore takes extraordinary risks;

195

—*Rationale.* Collectively constructing rationalizations to discount negative feedback or past failures.

—*Morality.* Believing unquestioningly in the inherent morality of the group and therefore being non-critical of decisions.

—*Stereotyping.* Assuming certain views and prejudices about the enemy".

—*Pressure.* Directing group pressure against any person expressing doubts and concern.

—*Self-censorship.* Talking oneself out of doubts or concerns and refraining from voicing them.

—*Unanimity.* Illusion that everyone agrees because no one voices dissent.

—*Mindguards.* Protecting each other and leader from adverse feedback and negative consequences of past decisions.

The way to avoid this deadly situation or to curb it if it is developing is for each member to actively assume the role of critical evaluator, and purposely remain impartial until *all* facts are in. It helps to encourage a "devil's advocate" in the group to raise questions, challenge ideas and test decisions. We must remind each other that creative tension is normal between the staff and board, and between members of a group when it is really functioning.

CONCLUSION:

To keep an institution alive and well takes love and caring—not just for people, but for the institution itself. John Gardner warns, "*A society decays when its institutions and individuals lose their vitality . . . in the ever-renewing society what matures is a system or framework within which continuous innovation, renewal and rebirth can occur . . . the last act of a dying institution is to get out a new and enlarged edition of the rule book.*"[21]

So we begin as individuals caring about people—not just the clients we serve, but the staff and volunteers who serve with us. That caring must extend to the institutions and organizations that enable our caring and reach out into society itself. To change a society takes this kind of outward vision. But caring must strengthen into commitment and commitment into action if we are to preserve and nurture one of the greatest forces for rebirth and renewal this nation has . . . voluntarism.

References

1. Jay, Anthony, *Management and Machiavelli,* Holt, Rinehart and Winston, Inc., 1967, p. 79.

2. Lindeman, Eduard C., "A Fantasy," written for and presented to the Volunteers Personnel Committee of the YWCA of New York City, 1952.

3. Naylor, Harriet H., *Volunteers Today: Finding, Training and Working With Them,* Dryden Assoc., 1967-73, p. 9.

4. Ibid, Introduction.

5. Ibid, p. 49.

6. Louden, J. Keith and Zusman, Jack, *The Effective Director in Action,* AMACOM, a Division of Am. Management Assoc., 1975.

7. Drucker, Peter, *Management: Tasks, Responsibilities, Practices,* Harper and Row, 1973-74, p. 628.

8. Ibid, p. 628.

9. Louden and Zusman, p. 135.

10. Ibid, p. 128-143.

11. Drucker, Louden and Zusman, Naylor.

12. Louden and Zusman, p. 158.

13. Hanson, Pauline L. and Marmaduke, Carolyn T., *The Board Member— Decision Maker,* Han/Mar Publications, 1974, P.O. Box 6143, Sacramento, Calif. 95860.

14. Naylor, p. 56.

15. Greenleaf, Robert, *The Institution As Servant,* Center for Applied Studies, 1972, p. 7.

16. Ibid, p. 34.

17. Koontz, Harold, and O'Donnell, Cyril, *Principles of Management,* Mcgraw-Hill, Inc., 1955-68, p. 739.

18. Jay, p. 28.

19. Quick, Thomas L., article "The Many Uses of Task Forces", *Personnel,* Jan.-Feb., 1974, Vol. 51, AMA Assoc.

20. Janis, Irving, article "Group Think" in *Psychology Today,* Nov., 1971.

21. Gardner, John, *Self-Renewal,* Harper & Row, 1963-64, p. 3, 5 & 55.